Answering The Call

Life Of A Helicopter Pilot In Vietnam And Beyond

Bob Grandin

16pt

Copyright Page from the Original Book

Copyright © Bob Grandin

First published 2019

Copyright remains the property of the authors and apart from any fair dealing for the purposes of private study, research, criticism or review, as permitted under the Copyright Act, no part may be reproduced by any process without written permission.

All inquiries should be made to the publishers.

Big Sky Publishing Pty Ltd
PO Box 303, Newport, NSW 2106, Australia
Phone: 1300 364 611
Fax: (61 2) 9918 2396
Email: info@bigskypublishing.com.au
Web: www.bigskypublishing.com.au

Cover design and typesetting: Think Productions

Proudly printed and bound in China by Hang Tai Printing Company Limited

 A catalogue record for this book is available from the National Library of Australia

For Cataloguing-in-Publication entry see National Library of Australia.

Creator: Bob Grandin
Title: Answering the Call: Life of a Helicopter Pilot in Vietnam and Beyond

TABLE OF CONTENTS

NEWSPAPER ARTICLES	ii
ACKNOWLEDGMENTS	iv
FOREWORD	vii
PROLOGUE	xii
CHAPTER 1: A TASTE OF ACTION	1
CHAPTER 2: OFF FOR SOME REAL ACTION	21
CHAPTER 3: ORIENTATION TO PHUOC TUY PROVINCE	44
CHAPTER 4: THE BATTLE OF LONG TAN	94
CHAPTER 5: SEARCHING FOR THE ENEMY	134
CHAPTER 6: STARTING THE CHANGEOVER	179
CHAPTER 7: COUNTDOWN	206
EPILOGUE	235
MORE GREAT READS	238
BACK COVER MATERIAL	254

I dedicate this book to all the veterans who 'Answered the Call' of duty and then struggle as they attempt to settle back into civilian life.

NEWSPAPER ARTICLES

'Watch from aloft', *The Sun*, 31 October 1966
'Next Stop Vietnam', *The Australian*, 24 May 1966
'The digger's best friend', *Canberra Times*, 7 September 1966
'Iroquois join Caribou in Vietnam', *RAAF News*, July 1966
'Baptism of fire for Iroquois', *RAAF News*, August 1966
'Vital Iroquois role in Viet battle', *RAAF News*, September 1966
'RAAF Heroism-'Copters turned tide of battle', Unknown paper, circa 22 August 1966
'Family Aid', *RAAF News*, August 1966
'Next move may be away', *The Sun*, 17 November 1966
'War against mosquitoes', *RAAF News*, December 1966
'Children ride in helicopters', *RAAF News*, December 1966
'Helicopter hero', *The Sun*, 15 Feb 1967
'Helicopters clash with Viet Cong', *RAAF News*, December 1966
'RAAF Carry Cong', *The Australian*, 8 April 1967
'Flying over the Delta', *RAAF News*, November 1966

'Our 'copters hit Cong river base', *The Sun*, 25 May 1967

'Pictures from Vietnam', *RAAF News*, November 1966

ACKNOWLEDGMENTS

The drive to write this book began after I had completed the manuscript for *"The Battle of Long Tan as told by the Commanders to Bob Grandin'* by Allen & Unwin. I commenced a Bachelor of Arts in Creative Writing at the University of the Sunshine Coast and in my third year enrolled in a unit that allowed me to focus on writing a manuscript. I initially transcribed my memory of day to day activity from my logbook, but my supervisor, Dr James Forsyth, encouraged me to expand the writing to include my life after Vietnam as he recognised a colourful, if troubled, set of experiences. My father, a Regular Army Major in the sixties, had saved news cuttings about me that appeared in the newspapers, despite my being with "the enemy-the RAAF" and he had also saved the RAAF News, that carried stories about Vietnam. I recognised that I could dovetail my experiences with these stories and I am thankful that he saved these cuttings. As I reworked the manuscript, I recognised that I should also align my flying with the names of various Operations that were being carried out by the Task Force. The use of Ian McNeill's *"To Long Tan: the Australian army and the Vietnam war 1950-1966"* allowed me to recognise the relationship between his descriptions of helicopter involvement and my logbook. I wish to acknowledge my Flight Commander in 9Sqn Vietnam, Laddie Hindley, who provided a mentoring and stabilising influence to my life.

I must acknowledge my long-suffering wife, who supported me in my many years of searching and unsettled existence. Together with my children, we explored several adventures that coloured our life, but did not provide the answers. Her understanding and acceptance have been critical to my realising my potential to write this story.

This book was the winner of the RAAF Biennial Heritage Literature Award 2018.

FOREWORD

This book by Bob Grandin is a very important manuscript. In an era in which we have become all too aware of the impact of war on the young men and women deployed on operations, Bob reminds us that the enduring impact of conflict is not a new phenomenon but one which has been with us for generations. Our returned servicemen and women all have a life after deployment, sometimes remaining in uniform, but for most, sooner or later, as civilians. They marry, have children, manage careers and have to deal with the challenges life brings. For many, the spectre of war is never far away. It hovers in the background, forever looking over their shoulder, sometimes as a benign presence, at other times something far more sinister. Appreciating this experience, knowing how different the effects can be for each individual person who has witnessed war is important for all of us to understand. Bob's story of his deployment to Vietnam flying Iroquois helicopters with the Royal Australian Air Force (RAAF) is a window for us to look through to gain an empathetic appreciation of the experience of our veterans.

The RAAF Iroquois deployment to the Vietnam War over the years 1966-71 was shaped by three factors, which all combined to influence the experience of Bob Grandin and that of his fellow aircrew of No 9 Squadron who first deployed into Vietnam in June 1966. The first factor was the relatively new nature of helicopter operations in the counter-insurgency operations so typical of that war. While the RAAF had in fact deployed a squadron of Iroquois to Malaya for operations against the communist terrorists during the years 1962-66, the low intensity nature of the conflict and the relatively benign operating environment did not truly provide significant lessons or provide a direction to guide further training and development of the use of helicopters in conflict. This is a salient point. The nature of the war in Vietnam was new to the RAAF, and this put pressure on the young aircrew like Bob to rapidly assess and adapt to the trying conditions of the counter-insurgency war.

While not the first wartime deployment of RAAF helicopters, when the personnel of No 9 Squadron arrived in Vietnam in 1966, they were to all intents and purposes entering into unknown territory. This situation was not helped by the second factor. The RAAF had began helicopter operations in 1947 in a role which could best be described as search, rescue and rear area logistics support. That the most prolific user of helicopters in the early years was the RAAF's Aircraft Research and Development Unit, would suggest that there had been only limited study since 1947 in the development of helicopters as a combat capability. This was also a characteristic of the senior officers of the RAAF at the time. As helicopters had only been a minor force component prior to the acquisition of the Iroquois in 1962, no helicopter aircrew had yet to reach a senior position within the Air Force who might have provided guidance from a position of authority. It was once again a necessity of the war that it would fall to the aircrew of No 9 Squadron to educate their senior command on the demands of rotary wing operations in conflict even as they themselves were learning.

The third factor which influenced No 9 Squadron's war was one common for all Australian units at the time. Our commitment to the war was small in comparison to the American effort. In 1966 US forces counted their helicopter fleets in the thousands, whereas Australia's was so small it was only able to commit eight Iroquois to the conflict. This was not an example of parsimony on the part of the RAAF, rather a reflection that there were simply no additional helicopters available to send. The small numbers of airframes meant that the tactics and large scale of operations suitable for US forces were simply out of reach for the far more modest Australian Task Force. Once again, it was the aircrew of No 9 Squadron who had to develop the plans and tactics suitable for small force operations.

The limitations and challenges faced by No 9 Squadron were not always appreciated by other elements deployed into theatre at the time. It was into this challenging environment of the conflict in Vietnam that Bob Grandin arrived in June 1966 as a young helicopter pilot. His story of that war and that of his later life is a worthy story and part of RAAF heritage. It was for this reason that Bob Grandin's *Answering the Call—My Life as a Helicopter Pilot in Vietnam and Beyond* is such a worthy winner of the 2018 RAAF Heritage Award for Literature.

Gavin Turnbull
Air Vice-Marshal
Deputy Chief of the Air Force
April 2019

'Watch from aloft', The Sun, 31 October 1966.

PROLOGUE

It seems so long ago and yet just yesterday. Now, after 50 years, a significant day for Australia in the war in Vietnam has become the subject of public debate as the commander at Long Tan continues to fight for recognition for his men, Delta Company, 6RAR, and those who supported them.

My first foray into remembering Vietnam days was writing a book published by Allen and Unwin with the title *The Battle of Long Tan: As told by the commanders to Bob Grandin*. It took seven years of remembering, transcribing, researching and vigorous discussion to produce a book about this eventful day on 18 August 1966. Three of us were invited to the Australian War Memorial in Canberra to give a presentation on the Battle of Long Tan. Bob Buick, a regular army sergeant who took charge of 11 Platoon after his commander was shot; Dave Sabben, a national service lieutenant commander of 10 Platoon; and me, a regular air force flight lieutenant pilot who flew in one of the ammunition resupply helicopters.

Our presentation of the minute-by-minute progression of events as seen by those in the forefront of the battle was enthusiastically received. The video of the presentation was a catalyst for others in command on the day, especially Harry Smith, the Company Commander, to gather together and work to produce a story from 'the sharp end'-accounts of their personal experiences as they commanded the battle troops. I was responsible for telling the helicopter story on behalf of the commander, Frank Riley, who had since passed away. Given my academic background and experience with writing other books I was given the role of bringing the individual contributions together into a coherent story.

In Australia, the war in Vietnam was not a popular war. Political differences of opinion were used to exploit the opportunity to divide the country on the value of our contribution. This mirrored activity in the USA. The use of conscripted youth became a very sensitive issue as the prospect of 'underage' men being unwillingly thrust into the line of fire created alarming images. At least the legal drinking age was lowered to allow these 'men' to drink alcohol.

The groundswell of resistance developed momentum throughout the years of the war. After more than 16 years, our longest ever involvement in a war at the time, and much bitter argument, the Opposition won government.

This provided a platform from which the efforts of those who fought in Vietnam could be belittled and almost disgraced. Rather than being greeted with the warmth that previous diggers had received upon their return from overseas conflicts, Vietnam veterans were 'blamed' for being involved and despised for the deeds of others.

The veterans who had experienced a most difficult type of war environment were forced to hide in shame. Many chose to move to an alternative form of existence. The compatriots with whom I wrote the book experienced unsettledness in work, broken marriages, anger and violence, illness-both physical and mental, and frequent withdrawal from society.

I began my life after Vietnam with an argumentative approach, which led to me leaving my career in the Royal Australian Air Force a few years after my return from the war. I embarked on a new career as a teacher in which I focused on unsettled students. I made frequent changes of work location. It was difficult to understand whether I was chasing a dream, looking for an idealistic environment, or frustrated by a loss of meaning in my life. I developed a general decline in my tolerance for others. I became a champion of the underdog and challenged the system that created divisions within our society.

My determination to develop alternative school climates took me well outside the established norms of my employer. While I achieved some international recognition, completed a Doctorate in Education on *Children's Experience of Learning in an Alternate School*, then later a Doctor of Philosophy on *The Crisis in Traditional Schooling*, the smaller alternative schools I created were closed on economic rationalist grounds by the establishment as they funded bigger traditional schools. Conservative bureaucratic stability failed to recognise the growing need to cater for diversity in a changing social environment.

My frustration overwhelmed me and it gradually became impossible for me to work in front of a class as my efforts to meet the needs of the students were thwarted by traditional school structures. The stresses of my past emerged and drained my ability to accept these frustrations. Luckily, at this time I was able to go to the USA and work in a university centre for learning, where the focus was on the needs of the learner in the classroom. This period also included the time of the attack on the Twin Towers on 911, which left a lasting impression. During the first few days, when all civilian aircraft ceased flying and an eerie silence crept over the suburbs as everyone stayed indoors, my feelings of being at war rose once again.

At night, the lights of fighter aircraft circling nuclear power plants created an image of intense danger. Our local postal exchange was the one through which anthrax was transmitted by post and we needed to use gloves when handling the mail. Tensions remained high as everything attempted to return to normal. A few months later, my wife returned to Australia and I followed after another six months. While I had the opportunity to remain for a longer period, I felt uneasy and desired the stability of home.

I returned to study, completing a degree in writing/communication as I felt a need to write, and it was at that time I commenced working on this book. I did some work through the university with socially and educationally disadvantaged young people and proceeded to do another degree in Psychology. I was also able to teach in a pre-service teacher education program for a few years, but my student-centred approach did not suit the curriculum delivery approach of the Education Department. Following an International Research Project on the Mental Health of School students in Australia and the UK, I did the PhD on the crisis in schools. I continued to tackle schooling issues on behalf of those young people excluded from school as the conveyor belt approach discarded them as faulty products.

But returning to our book on Long Tan, not only did it give the personal experiences of those who fought on the day, but the stories of their lives before and after Vietnam. The youthful exuberance of a group of post-World War II boys evolved into a group of frustrated veterans for whom honour and recognition had been belittled. All suffer from the physical and mental ailments of intensive battle. The book also challenges many of the myths that arose about the battle and raises the injustices that have been perpetrated with the recognition for those who fought so valiantly.

After 36 years the first of these injustices was reversed as our book moved onto the bookshelves-South Vietnamese awards that had been given were now allowed to be worn. Finally, some awards were changed back to those Harry Smith had recommended after being downgraded by higher authority at the time and further recognition provided to some individuals. More generic recognition for the support elements of the day remains an issue of recognition for Harry Smith.

My role in the Battle of Long Tan was small – albeit highly significant – and I have felt the need to work through the experiences of my whole year of flying helicopters in Vietnam. The demons that frustrate me as I try to find the real value of my life's work delude me into thinking that I did not do anything significant during that year. Yet the headlines and history books illustrate that my squadron and I did amazing things during this time. This confusion reflects the way that PTSD creeps into your life and colours the way you think and act.

This book is the journey of my exploration through my subconscious as I recall the extreme situations I experienced in war, the impact of suppressing wartime events into the subconscious, and the truth of my involvement in the Battle of Long Tan.

CHAPTER 1

A TASTE OF ACTION

At dawn on 1 June 1965, I sat at the end of the runway in Lae, Papua New Guinea, in a Neptune P2V Maritime Reconnaissance bomber. This aircraft, developed during World War II, had a new life in a long-range reconnaissance role. Her two turbo-charged piston engines had been supplemented by two jet engines to allow her to take off with a very heavy fuel load. We were about to depart and escort the troop-carrying HMAS *Sydney* on her first journey to the war in Vietnam.

Fully armed with active torpedoes and fuelled with 3,850 gallons (16,000 litres) of fuel, we were ready to fly into a 'war' situation on Operation Trimdon. I opened the throttles on the two jets to maximum for the skipper, Bill. They screamed as they thirstily drank into the fuel supplies. I then brought the two supercharged piston engines to maximum power. Bill stood on the brakes as the aircraft shuddered and struggled to leap forward under the thrust of the four-bladed propeller.

'Here goes,' he said over the intercom, and released the brakes.

'Here comes the first barrel,' Bill said.

'Sixty-six, sixty-seven, sixty-eight, sixty-nine.' I called out the speed. We wanted 70 knots at this point. The deep groan of the engines was gradually gaining that sound that told us they were winning the battle to get the old girl up to speed.

'We need 80 at the next one or it's abort.' Would we really be able to stop if she didn't get up to speed? The aircraft continued to struggle to gain enough momentum. All the crew were willing it to fly.

'Seventy-eight, seventy-nine, eighty.'

'Let's hope our calculations were right as there is no stopping now,' Bill said as we watched the end of the runway looming up fast. It looked awfully close. The aircraft was starting to jump into the air as we hit the bumps in the runway.

Bill pushed forward on the control column to hold the aircraft down on the runway to get as much speed as he could, but as the end of the runway started to disappear under us he needed to nurse her into the air. The runway ended on a small escarpment that fell away to the water below. She groaned and then clanged away as the undercarriage folded up into place. There was a sense of sinking as we soared over the edge of the cliff and passed an old shipwreck sticking out of the water. But she was flying, seemingly on a cushion of air just above the water. We let her cruise along just above the water until she gained a comfortable speed.

'Holy shit, that was close,' said Jeff, better known as Big Black, one of the navigators.

'Well done, skipper,' said Pete, the lead electronics operator and an old mate of Bill's.

'How about a coffee?' Bill coolly called over the intercom.

'Roger, skip,' responded one of the signallers from down in the galley.

Our adventure had started this way as we needed to carry as much fuel as possible to give us maximum time on station escorting the convoy. Lae did not have a long airstrip and to make things harder the temperature and humidity were very high. This created a high density altitude that significantly reduced the performance of the engines. We needed to study our performance charts very closely to determine the maximum weight our aircraft could be and still take off in the length of runway available.

A well-drilled plan of speeds and distance as we progressed down the runway was devised. We measured the strip in a jeep and placed markers along the side at our critical points. This plan was necessary if we were to get safely into the air. Or, if we had to abandon the take-off, to stop before the end. In some ways it was lucky that the airstrip ended at a small cliff over the sea, without any obstacles. When you peered down the runway it looked very short. But this was a 'live' action situation and a time to test our professional ability to gain the maximum performance from our aircraft.

This 'real' war was brewing in South-East Asia and the USA had committed troops to supporting the South Vietnamese government against the communist insurgency from the north. The Australian Government decided to provide a Battalion of troops to fight with the US 1st Cavalry out of Ben Hoa, near Saigon. They were to be transported to Vietnam aboard HMAS *Sydney*, a converted aircraft carrier. International intelligence indicated that the Russians were not happy with this involvement. They may have been prepared to use their submarine fleet to sink this ship on its way through the South China Sea.

It was decided that it would be escorted by anti-submarine aircraft, as well as destroyers, on its journey. My crew was allocated the passages between Papua New Guinea and the Philippines, operating out of Lae in PNG. As I was a junior captain, Bill, a senior captain, was assigned to the 13-man crew to guide us through the intensity and seriousness of the operation. Our aircraft was loaded with torpedos that actively sought out underwater targets and had explosive warheads capable of sinking a submarine.

We positioned in Lae, awaiting our turn to escort the Sydney. Everyone was excited about the operation. It was that curious conundrum where intelligent young men willingly put their lives at risk for a cause. A service man trains for action, often involving a kill or be-killed scenario, and feels fulfilled when given the opportunity to test his level of skill. We were entering our first test. The conversation was tinged with the uneasy realisation that an attack could be an action that started another world war.

We flew northeast out of Lae to our rendezvous point with the ships. The crew of the current escorting aircraft radioed that they were leaving station and that there was nothing to report. We flew over the three ships, two destroyers escorting the aircraft carrier, and established radio contact. Then we set up a creeping-line-ahead search pattern along the course the ships would take.

Convoy escort had the potential to be a very boring time with little action. Each crew station was manned on a rotational basis, with those off-station sleeping, eating or relaxing looking out a window. On this trip there was an air of expectancy and the added tension of 'the real thing'.

'Contact. Surface vessel 345 degrees 65 miles (100 kilometres),' suddenly rang out from Pete, the radar operator. Everyone became alert. Although it was unlikely to be a submarine on the surface, we could not be sure. It also had the potential to be a torpedo gunboat.

'Head 340 degrees, time to run 24 minutes,' was the response from Big Black.

'Roger, heading 340. Standby stations,' Bill called, preparing the crew for action. 'What does the contact look like, Pete?'

'Just something small I would say,' he replied.

'I won't arm the torpedoes unless he disappears from the screen,' Bill stated. 'Keep a sharp watch in case it is a submarine and it dives.'

'I have him; turn 3 degrees port,' called Johnny, the attack radar operator.

'I can see a small cargo ship,' said Frank from the nose observer position.

'Standby to take photographs, Waist. Radio, send the position to com centre,' Bill commanded.

I let out a sigh of relief and could feel the more relaxed tenor in the conversation of the crew over the intercom. We headed back into the search pattern.

We picked up a couple of merchant ships and four fishing vessels on our radar over the next few hours. We flew over each one, photographed them and plotted their position, before reporting them to maritime headquarters in Sydney, who were controlling the whole operation. The crew continued rotations of being on station and going down the back for some rest and a bite to eat.

We sprang into action again when Johnny called over the intercom that he had picked up a target on the radar that disappeared after three sweeps. 'Take us there,' Bill called to Black.

Pete had been looking over Johnny's shoulder and Bill asked him what he thought. 'It was a definite contact, skipper, and it's gone now.'

'OK, time to run, Black?'

'About 12 minutes, Skip.'

'OK, everyone, action stations. I'm arming the torpedos and will open the Bombay doors 2 miles out. Do you have anything on the attack radar, John?'

'No, all clear,' Johnny replied.

'Coming up over the top,' Black called.

'OK, let's initiate a MAD (magnetic anomaly detector) circle with buoys and let's see if there is anything down there,' Bill commanded.

'Smoke and buoy gone,' John called from the waist.

We circled for 15 minutes without any sign of a contact.

'Let's drop a percussion bomb at the next buoy and see if he's hiding in the middle,' Bill said.

'No echo,' came from Murph.

'Time to call it off,' Bill said. 'Notify the ships of this position and that we have not had any further contact. Put us back on the creeping-line-ahead pattern, Murph.' Frank had taken over on the nav table.

We returned to our routines as we transitioned through the Straits.

It was 1.30 in the afternoon when there was a call over the intercom.

'ECM contact bearing 240 degrees.'

Curley had been scanning suspected submarine frequencies and had picked up a signal. Unfortunately, the ECM (electronic counter measures) only provides a line along which the radar signal travels; the target could be any distance up or down that line.

I was flying at the time and turned the plane onto a heading of 240 degrees, or south-west. Bill came rushing back to the cockpit and kicked the copilot out of his seat. He had been having a meal down the back. All the crew moved to action stations and prepared to hunt down the submarine.

'What did you get, Curley?' Bill asked.

'Just two sweeps in the low frequency band; I couldn't identify the exact frequency in that time.'

'OK, we'll assume it's a sub. Pete, radio Sydney and tell them. Bob, call the ships and report a possible submarine contact and that we are investigating. How far in front of them are we, Black? Everyone, keep your eyes open.'

Big Black put us about 35 nautical miles in front of the ships. We had a couple of hours to find the submarine before they got to our location. The ships' operations centre responded they would be moving to evasive action and for us to keep them informed. This meant that the two destroyers would move into a crisscrossing course in front of the carrier using their sonar to search for the submarine. The carrier also started a zigzag course so that it did not provide an easy target.

'Let's drop a sonar buoy every 5 nautical miles (8 kilometres) and see if we can hear him under the water. I'm arming the torpedoes. How far do you think his radar would travel, Curley?' Bill rattled off his commands and questions.

'Up to 40 miles,' Curley replied.

'All right. We'll go 50 miles and turn around to travel back up the line. Got that, Black?' Bill responded, getting the navigator to plot our course along the original line of bearing of the radar intercept.

'Hey, chief, what happens if this bugger pops up on the surface and has a gun, or fires a missile at us?' Johnny, one of the radar operators, asked. We didn't have any rockets or guns, just torpedoes designed to get a submarine under the water.

'We might have to drop a sonar buoy on the gunner's head,' he joked. 'But I don't think they'd be game enough to do that; they don't know we don't have any rockets on board.'

'What happens if we find this guy, do we just go in and sink him? Shit, if we did that it could turn the cold war into a hot one,' I said across the cockpit to Bill.

'We don't have any choice. If he's here we assume he's hostile and intends to sink the bloody carrier,' he responded.

'Hearing anything on the sonar buoys, John?' Bill asked.

'Nope,' he responded.

'Anything on radar?'

'I don't have any targets except the ships.'

'We've travelled 50 miles from our first contact; turn onto 060 degrees. How far do you want to go in this direction?' Black asked.

'We'll go out 50 again from the original point of contact,' he said. The ECM bearing could have come from either direction along the line.

The crew were all talking to each other. A real sense of nervousness had moved over them. You could also read the excitement of the chase in their expressions. After all, if we found and sunk this submarine we would be heroes, even if we were the ones to trigger a new world war. Everyone who was not at a piece of equipment was scanning the horizon for any visual signs; say the feather of spray that a periscope makes in the water, or even the sub on the surface.

We turned again and went back down the line. The ships were now in sight, zigging and zagging their way along. Over the next couple of hours they moved through the danger area and continued on their way towards the South China Sea. We kept travelling back and forward along the line until we recognised that the ships were far enough ahead of the danger area. We then joined the search ahead of the ships for another hour before we returned to Lae.

We were disappointed that we had not caught the submarine. We were relieved that we had not started another war. We were pleased that the ships had been able to transit our area of responsibility safely. But then we spent a lot of the return journey trying to solve the dilemma of what we had seen on the ECM.

We got the answer in the 'wash-up' of the whole operation. Operations officers from the squadrons took all the aircraft logbooks to a debriefing at naval headquarters in Sydney. These indicated all the actions of the navigators, radar and radio operators. Contacts were cross-correlated with these books. It became evident that one of our squadron's crews had been transiting to Manila to take up its station, passing over our search area, and the operator had tested his attack radar for two sweeps to relieve the boredom. We were commended for intercepting the signal, but it was deflating to realise that we had been chasing a phantom submarine.

Our next challenge was to get back into Lae as it was approaching dark and there were showers in the area. As we came into the bay leading into the airport Johnny was on the attack radar and lining us up on the shipwreck just off the end of the runway.

'Can anyone see the strip?' Bill asked.

'Not yet,' came from several stations.

'Coming up over the wreck,' said Johnny.

'Can't see it,' was the initial response.

'There it is, under the right wing.'

'We're over the beach, skip.'

'I have it,' Bill called. 'Hang on,' as he planted the old girl solidly down on the runway and jumped on the brakes.

Little did I know at this time that in one year exactly I would be transiting to the Vietnam War. This taste of action was to mean that I was only too keen to volunteer to transfer to helicopters when an air force-wide call went out.

There was action in the air and, no matter where it was, I was itching to be a part of it.

WHAT DRIVES ONE TO VOLUNTEER TO GO TO WAR?

It's so difficult to appreciate the forces that make a young man confront the challenges of world peace and its converse, war.

I had joined the air force after a life growing up in a military family. My adolescence was spent on a huge army base that was a disposals centre for war surplus weapons from World War II. There were hundreds and hundreds of big guns, trucks, tanks and other weapons. Regular auctions were attended by scrap metal merchants and disposal agents. Each was given a wired compound in which to keep their purchases before they were transported away. We invaded these compounds and played the roles of tank commander or artillery gunner. It was a natural progression for us to take on the defence of the nation from our fathers, who had all fought in World War II.

A steady flow of recruits lined up to join the army, navy and air force during this era. It was very competitive to gain a place in the more elite elements of these services. But it promised a life of adventure, challenge, a high level of skills training and pride in being chosen to defend your country in the next war. To volunteer to fight was a natural outcome of the adventure associated with a life in the defence forces.

It was also the place to receive the most advanced training and vocational skills. Military applications of an innovation normally preceded its use in civilian life. For example, colour television displays were widely used for weapon systems in the pilot's cockpit well before it was available on our TV sets. Military technicians were highly valued tradesmen. Flying in the service was to 'use' an aircraft rather than the 'bus driving' associated with commercial aviation.

As a boy, I was excited by the valour and daring of the fighter pilots in the Battle of Britain. I read the stories of Biggles, Captain WE Johns' fictional wartime pilot, whose adventures involved outflying his German counterpart and saving the day. I imagined myself in his role, a dashing risk-taker who was invincible through his superior flying skill. As I grew up I saw aircraft evolve from being driven by piston engines to being propelled by jet engines to ever higher speeds. It looked to be an exciting future and I wanted to be part of it.

The enemy was clear cut in my mind. It was the Germans and the Japanese. Despite their defeat, history had placed them in the roles of the enemy. We needed to be wary of their rise again. However, by the time I had left school and joined the air force we were fighting the communists. The USSR (Union of Soviet Socialist Republics) had emerged as the leader of a socialist movement that followed a Marxist philosophy aimed to free the underclass of the world from imperialism and capitalism. They saw it as a natural progression that the workers of the world would unite and overthrow the capitalist employers so that all might share in the benefits of production. But as George Orwell satirized in his book *Animal Farm* the realities of power rarely saw an equal sharing of outcomes.

The Western world decided that communism was a loss of democratic right for the people that it purported to free. A cold war developed as the two major forces, the USSR and the USA, confronted each other with more and more threatening retaliatory weapons. Hot spots of conflict broke out, initially in Korea. The first of many conflicts ensued with each side facing the other in 'limited' conflict, a term coined to indicate the non-use of atomic weapons.

Social attitudes in the 1950s were that any aggressor must be confronted and defeated as people recalled the experience of the two world wars. Those of us in the service were very comfortable seeing the threat of communism as the challenge for our future. We were the operational arm of the defence planning organisation which, in turn, implemented government policy. Close links were drawn for us between the evil of German and Japanese forces and the potential excesses of the communists. News reports of the suppression and murder of those daring to oppose the communist regimes started to become plentiful.

As this influence moved southwards through Asia, one of our northern neighbours,

Indonesia, aligned itself with communism. Our defence plans were built around meeting this threat from Indonesia. However, not everyone believed in the evil of socialism and, in fact, the left elements of the Labor Party aligned themselves with this philosophy. They established a groundswell of opposition to military intervention in what they determined was the internal struggle to determine which political party should rule a country. This, together with the bad experiences troops had had in Korea, caused a reduction in the recruitment levels of the services. The perceived growing threat from Indonesia meant that the idea of conscription was debated and then passed in parliament to strengthen the numbers in the forces.

The move from a volunteer force ignited the voices of protest. There were those who had an empathy with the socialist agenda. Both in the USA and in Australia a movement mobilised that opposed the use of force to counter the spread of communist influence. A very significant social division occurred that was to lead to major, and sometimes violent, protest.

I was to miss much of this protest as I was in Vietnam by the time it grew to a significant size and I then spent two further years serving in Malaysia. I was satisfied that the threat to Australian democracy was real, that to fight before the threat reached your own shores was sound policy, and that supporting our major ally was a natural progression of defence treaties we had signed for our own benefit. The strange logic of servicemen, which justified war as the extension of the years of training, moved into gear. Each skill was honed to a fine edge so that one would have the upper hand in any fight.

When I felt like Biggies, I could take to the air and defend my country, whose citizens would be eternally grateful. Or so I thought. There was no foresight of the terror of jungle warfare, the horror of the injuries that occur in guerrilla conflicts, or the lack of support from a population that had become deeply divided over the right to be involved in the conflict at all.

'Next Stop Vietnam', The Australian, 24 May 1966.

What caused the emotional and physical debilitation that became a major outcome for so many who fought in Vietnam? Was it the real images of the experience, the imagined nightmares of what could have happened, the lack of emotional support from a community that they were sent to defend, or the very limited psychological services that help phase service people back into a community following a traumatic experience?

For some, the degeneration into substance abuse enabled a form of escape from the experience. Many tried to hide the memories in the back of their minds. As time progressed, more and more individuals presented with an altered emotional state and behaviour that was difficult to predict.

By 1984 enough evidence had been collected to indicate that there was a problem and it was named post-traumatic stress disorder (PTSD) at a medical conference in Hawaii. While the disorder was not limited to war experience, there was no doubt that frontline battle images sharply heightened the onset and a real fear for one's life had a critical impact. When the disorder would present itself was highly variable in both intensity and time. Even for the most confident of us the loss of ability to cope with stress gradually arose.

CHAPTER 2

OFF FOR SOME REAL ACTION

We arrived from all around our air force to reinforce 9 Squadron. Some others had been recruited from the Royal Air Force in England. Those from overseas were experienced helicopter pilots on four-year short service commissions: Phil with his big moustache and Pommie sense of humour; Ted the quiet one; Bill G with his tribe of kids; and big, tall Fred. They were mature aged (around 40 years old) pilots looking to continue flying. Some of our guys had a similar desire. Mike had flown in World War II but had flown a desk for too many years; he wanted to be back in the air. Geoff B had years of experience in maritime and wanted a change. I was a young 25-year-old who came from the other maritime squadron looking for adventure.

Geoff B did not have married quarters allocated to him, so I offered his family a caravan in our backyard. He and his wife Margaret plus their children Leanne and Ian lived there for the next few months.

Our conversion to helicopters began with ground school. The new terminology-rotary wing, cyclic, collective, directional control pedals, hover, transition, autorotation-was introduced and explained. The intricacies of the jet engine with its constant speed fuel controls; the rotor and its momentum to create the lift for flying; the collective and cyclic plates and their twisting of the rotor to produce movement; and, the tail rotor with its counter-balancing role. We quickly learned that the aerodynamics of the helicopter and the aeroplane were very dissimilar.

We started helicopter flight training at the beginning of February 1966 and I was assigned Athol as my instructor. He was a tall, prematurely balding character with a sadistic sense of humour. He was a good instructor because he allowed you to find out things for yourself, which provided the basis for his humour and jokes. He would maintain a dry dialogue about the lack of control I was exhibiting and the unusual 'attitudes' of the helicopter that people would be seeing. But he insisted that you struggle with the situation and solve it yourself.

Athol watched me over-controlling; that is, moving the control stick, called the cyclic lever, around more than necessary to achieve the required response.

'How do you stop this bloody thing from jumping all over the place?' I retorted.

He just smiled and took hold of my wrist, placing it on my knee.

'Now just grab it with your thumb and forefinger and just move them.'

'Shit, that makes a huge difference. Why didn't you tell me before?'

'Not everyone's as ham-fisted as you are, and it makes for a good laugh to watch you fighting the helicopter,' he said with a smile from ear to ear.

The difference was unbelievable; the wrist braced on the knee acted as a stabiliser, and I quickly realised that everyone else flew that way. Nothing like the huge control movements in a Neptune or a 'Goonie Bird' (DC3 Dakota) I had previously experienced. It was amazing how responsive the helicopter was to slight movements, which was essential when operating in close proximity to the ground, people or obstacles.

The Bell UH 1B Iroquois helicopter was a light, fidgety flying machine with hydraulic assisted controls that required a feather-light touch. Added to that, the helicopter was an unstable platform, so you had to hold the control at all times; to let go was to court disaster as the helicopter would instantly assume an unusual attitude.

Initially Athol took me up to altitude to get used to handling the controls, well away from the ground. Moving the cyclic lever forward made the helicopter move forward at an increasing speed; backwards slowed a moving helicopter down and caused a stationary one to go backwards. Moving it left made the helicopter move laterally to the left; similarly, right moved the helicopter to the right. All these movements tilted the cyclic plate that then varied the angle of the blades as each one passed the direction you had chosen, creating an imbalance in lifting vector, which created the movement of the helicopter. To remain stationary the cyclic lever needed to be in the central position.

Tilting of the main rotor, which occurred with any of these movements, meant a reduction of the vertical lifting force and so the helicopter also began to descend. Just imagine the slightest movement of the lever in your hand causing movement in three dimensions. The lever in your left hand that was pivoted at the rear beside your seat, called the collective lever, controlled vertical movement. Raising the collective lever caused the angle on both the blades of the rotor to increase so there was an increase in the lifting force and the helicopter would ascend. Lowering it had the opposite effect. So as you moved the cyclic lever you also moved the collective lever, just a little bit, to maintain height.

Once I had these two levers relatively coordinated Athol made me also put my feet on the pedals situated out in the perspex dome in front of me. Any change in the collective had an associated change of power. Although the fuel flow was automatically controlled, the torque effect of this change of power was not. This torque effect caused the helicopter to rotate in the opposite direction around its centre. Directional control was achieved by foot pedals, which changed the angle of the blades on the tail rotor and caused a rotation left or right about the central axis.

Now I had three things to move in unison if I was to have control of my helicopter. For a pilot of old heavy aeroplanes, the hardest thing to learn was that movements of the helicopter controls needed to be 'feather' touches in contrast to the 'large' movements I was used to.

So, movement of the cyclic to move off forward also required a lifting of the collective to maintain height or to climb away and a movement of the foot pedals to maintain direction. The challenge of operating a helicopter was to coordinate these movements in a smooth and controlled manner. It was certainly a challenge for me and I often wonder whether I ever achieved a 'fine' touch.

'This is not a mix-master,' Athol would say. 'You don't have to beat the thing. Relax and caress the controls, it'll be much more enjoyable.'

Finally, I had sufficient control for Athol to be willing to take me near the ground. The first experience close to the ground, as I tried to hover the helicopter over a spot, illustrated just how difficult it was to keep steady. Athol started at a safe height, maybe a couple of metres, but gradually brought me down to a few centimetres above the ground.

'How can you just sit there,' I would say, 'when I'm going to kill us both?'

'Now just relax, Robert,' he would reply, 'It's all in the fingers.'

Or if I was making a mess of it.

'Keep your bloody wrist still! Use your fingers.'

Then I would know I was worrying him and start to panic more. He would take over and say, 'Now start again.'

Close to the ground the movement seemed exaggerated and the sense of imminent danger rose in your mind. That Athol could just sit there and watch was incredible to me. He was extremely quick to take over though if I slipped back into over-controlling.

It was essential to master a hover at this height so you could 'land' the helicopter on a pad without too much clatter. The steel runners under the helicopter did not provide any form of absorbing pad during the landing.

An incident that occurred during this phase illustrates Athol's sense of humour. I was struggling to keep the helicopter still before setting it down. Athol was insisting that I keep it a couple of centimetres above the landing pad.

'I see Jan [my wife] is watching,' he suddenly said to me.

The helicopter began to tap-dance as first one point of one skid hit the ground and then each of the other points seemed to hit in cyclic rotation. After a desperate effort to control this movement, in which I only over-controlled and exaggerated the movement, I lowered the collective and unceremoniously plopped onto the ground. A most embarrassing example of how I was progressing with the challenge of achieving three-dimensional control of this beast called a helicopter.

'Will you tell Jan that was a good landing?' he said sarcastically.

The next thing I learned was how to react if the engine stopped. In a fixed wing aircraft you pulled the nose back and converted speed to height and then glided to a safe landing spot.

In the helicopter you pushed the nose forward so the rotor continued to spin and maintained its momentum. You looked down between your feet and chose the best spot to land, because you were going almost straight down. You maintained the momentum in the rotor so that at about 100 feet (30 metres) you could raise the collective lever and turn this momentum into a lifting force that stopped the downward motion and allowed you to settle nicely onto the ground. This procedure was called autorotation. Initially it was a terrifying experience, plummeting to earth like a brick with one calculated chance to stop ending up in a pile of twisted metal.

As you learned to do it well you realised that it was a safer outcome than in a fixed wing aircraft as you did not have any forward speed as you came into contact with the ground. But it certainly took some getting used to, reacting in the opposite way to all your previous training and nervously waiting for just the right moment to 'pull pitch' (raise the collective lever) to stop the almost vertical descent.

By the middle of February I was allowed to go solo. Bluey, one of the intrepid trainee crewmen/door-gunners came along to keep me company. We flew around the airstrip doing a couple of approaches and some hovering practice.

Once we had gained control in open spaces it was necessary to learn to handle the helicopter in restricted spaces and amongst obstacles. There was a range of landing pads cleared amongst trees in the training area. We spent many hours practising approaching these from all sorts of directions and heights in preparation for operational activity.

'Where's the wind coming from? Watch you tail rotor, it's dragging in the trees. Slow down first, then descend into the clearing. Watch the tip of your rotors. Look out for that stump,' rattled off Athol's tongue, while my dazed mind wondered what to look at next.

Slowly but surely it became second nature and the ability to watch everything while gliding into the clearing became a part of the thrill of flying a helicopter.

When we were in the training area one form of activity that allowed us to practise hovering was collecting the bountiful quantities of mushrooms. A crewman would hang out of the helicopter with a knife and harvest mushrooms as we hovered from 'fairy ring' to 'fairy ring' around the paddock.

We moved on to learn how to carry sling loads below the helicopter.

'The first essential action is to touch the ground shortly before moving in for the sling hook-up,' Athol instructed me. 'This is to release the static electricity generated by the rotor as it whirls through the air.'

'If you forget,' Bluey commented from the back-he was going to do the hook-up, 'I will get one hell of a jolt. If I come flying out the side, you have to do the next hook-up and we will show you what it's bloody like.'

'Does it hurt?'

'It's all voltage and no amperage,' he said. 'It's not life threatening, but it's shocking,' he finished with a grin.

'Just as important to the guy underneath is that you hold steady, so he doesn't have to keep ducking his head. The sling hook is pretty heavy and awkward to handle. It's disconcerting enough for him having a helicopter centimetres above his head as he connects the hook, without having to be continuously bobbing up and down to avoid the bottom of the helicopter. Most are pretty quick in and out as they don't like it under there much.'

Similarly, when I was learning to use the winch it was essential to develop techniques that allowed me to keep the helicopter relatively stationary. This allowed the winch operator to guide the lifting sling to the patient below without it moving all over the place. Considering most winch operations were also to be carried out amongst trees or obstacles that prevented the helicopter from landing, it was essential that the line did not become entangled on one of them and cause a disaster.

The sensation that started to develop was one of three-dimensional control. You realised that you could go anywhere, up, down, forwards, backwards, and any combination of the above. It was a sensation of being able to fly, literally. The most critical lesson to be learned from this freedom was one of not abusing it. Flying low placed you closer to obstacles like power lines. Getting too close to large obstacles could interfere with the airflow through the rotor and create forces that drew you uncontrollably towards the object. Loose objects on the ground could be drawn up into the airflow through the rotor and create damage to the blades, or be sucked into the jet engine intake, creating a malfunction. But there was no denying the feeling of having a machine strapped to your body that allowed you to go anywhere, to move with three-dimensional freedom, or even dance if you wanted to.

We continued to fly several times a day in a hectic training schedule. We had been warned that an announcement would be made by the Prime Minister on the evening of 8 March 1966 and Geoff B and I were sitting on the front porch enjoying a beer with our wives, listening to parliament on the radio. After a lengthy introduction on Australia's duties and responsibilities in assisting our allies in opposing the spread of communism, Prime Minister Harold Holt outlined the nature of the extra commitment. We listened intently, waiting expectantly for him to include the helicopter squadron. We were last on the list.

'You beauty, we're going.'

'Looks like we have our chance, love,' Geoff B said to Marg.

'I'm not so sure I'm pleased,' Marg said. 'What about the danger?'

'Not as bad as driving down the road,' Geoff B replied.

'Don't a lot of people get killed?' Jan asked.

'No,' I said. 'We have vastly superior equipment and aircraft and there is no opposition air force. So it's relatively safe.'

'Casualty reports have been light,' Geoff B said.

'We'll be alright,' I said. 'Just need to see if we're on the list at the briefing tomorrow.'

To Geoff and I it was an opportunity to practise what we had trained for. It was not a sombre departure into a war zone where many were expected to die. After all, the allies would be in control of the country in no time!

Both Geoff B and I were on the list of 13 pilots to go in the first wave.

Not that everyone was keen to volunteer. Pilots started to resign their commissions rather than join the squadrons going to Vietnam. Don, my lead navigator from Maritime, had done a pilot's course. He was posted to the squadron and chose to resign rather than go.

I met him in the bar and chided him over the action.

'What's the matter, mate? Gutless?' I started.

'Fuck you,' he replied. 'Why do I need to go and fight some stupid Yank war? If that idiot Holt wants to "go all the way with LBJ" then let him go and die for the cause.'

'But don't you see the adventure? The thrill of battle? Beating shit out of the commies?'

'You fucking hero. What's the use if some shit shoots you?' Don bit back. 'I didn't do a pilot's course to become cannon fodder in a dubious war.'

'But surely you recognise that the odds are in our favour?'

'Big deal.'

'What about communism? Surely you don't want them to overrun the place,' I said as I started to justify our involvement.

'Fucking domino theory,' he replied. 'How the fuck are they going to get their hordes across the sea? They don't have a navy. They fuckin' can't swim either, for that matter. One minute we are conscripting kids to defend the country against Indonesia and the next we are diverting them to Vietnam. Now 18-year-olds are off to a bloody war. How many of them are going to die? In a war that has a dubious basis. I ask you?'

'You sound like the Labor Party. Been reading that shit that Cairns has been writing? If we don't fight them there, we have to fight them somewhere else. They won't be satisfied until they get thumped.'

We decided to part company agreeing to differ in our views. He went off to Qantas, earning lots of money, and I served my country for a medal or two.

I never doubted that a part of my role was to fight for my country whenever the government deemed it was necessary. My fellow squadron members never spoke of dissent in being sent and accepted the theory that it was better to fight overseas before the threat arrived in your country. We also believed that the freedom of Australian society was worth fighting for and we did not wish it to change to a communist ideology. Similarly, we were happy to support our allies in their time of need. It was all very patriotic, but a relatively normal attitude of most servicemen before the Vietnam War.

We began to prepare to go to war. Athol drove me on into advanced and then operational phases of our training. It was all very real and there was little time. By the end of March we had finished our conversion course; two very intensive months. In early April we prepared for an operational exercise, with 6RAR (Sixth Battalion Royal Australian Regiment) one of the battalions we would be supporting.

It was planned for the Shoalwater Bay area, north of Rockhampton, and this was to be the first, and only, time we would get to work with the troops. It took nine hours of flying time to get to Rocky, with an overnight stop at Amberley, near Brisbane. This is a long time in a vibrating machine that you must control all the time, unlike being able to use an auto-pilot in a fixed wing aircraft.

The training area was in the tropics, so it was hot and humid like we would encounter in Vietnam. There were hills, plains and mangrove swamps, also similar to the province that we would be operating in. We also had to contend with the mosquitoes and sandflies of the area. It provided a reasonable introduction to what we had to expect overseas. Although the crocodiles would not be in Vietnam.

We moved the troops from one place to another, trying to get quick and efficient embarking and disembarking procedures going. It turned out that the pressures of the enemy's presence made all these things happen so much faster. We also provided resupply missions, in which we took food and supplies to the troops in remote locations. Athol flew with me on several occasions to continue my training. Fifteen flying hours later we were deemed ready for war!

A memorable moment during this exercise was when, just like picking mushrooms, we used the helicopter to access the mangrove swamps and catch some mud crabs, big ones.

Our return journey was via Gladstone, Maryborough and Amberley, where we stayed overnight. The weather down the east coast was poor, especially inland. We were determined to get home. We had little enough time left with our wives, so we planned to travel down the coastline in the light aircraft corridor. The journey to Williamtown RAAF Base was not too bad as we were able to remain in visual contact with the ocean below. However, the weather over Sydney was particularly bad with intensive rain.

We decided to get some real tactical training and requested special permission to transit through Sydney air traffic control area. We set off and I was flying with Ted, one of the RAF pilots. It was typical English weather for him. But it got so intense that we had to land on the beach at The Entrance and wait for the storm to pass. It must have been quite a shock to those watching the rough seas in the storm to suddenly see six helicopters appear out of the gloom and land on the beach.

I moved to the lead helicopter with Tommy and became the radio link to Sydney air traffic control.

'Albatross formation, this is Sydney, could you identify your location? We do not have you on radar.'

'Sydney, this is Albatross, we are off Manly beach,' I replied. 'But we are below the height of the cliffs, in visual contact with the ground.'

We had slowed to a speed which maintained our visibility through the rain, often only 20 or 30 knots (30-50 kph). Slowly but surely we progressed south.

'Sydney, Albatross, we are entering through the heads; request clearance to fly up the harbour.'

'Roger, Albatross, are you visual? ... I have you now on radar 12nm on 025 degrees.'

'Roger, Sydney, we have visual contact with the control tower.'

The cloud was starting to lift to the south and we were able to proceed to Kingsford Smith Airport in Sydney.

Luckily, the weather between Sydney and Canberra was clearing. We could get back to Canberra. To any Sydneysiders looking out their windows it must have been a sight to see this long line of helicopters meandering along in the rain.

After 125 hours of flight training and 4 months I was off to Vietnam, where the squadron developed the majority of its tactical flying operations in a form of 'on the job training'.

I packed my tin trunk with a couple of uniforms, three flying suits, flying boots and helmet plus a couple of changes of civvies (non-uniform casual clothes). We couldn't take any electrical gear as the voltage was 110, not 240 as in Australia. So, with toilet gear and a few books to read added, the trunk was pretty light.

During the two weeks pre-embarkation leave Jan, my son Brett and I went to see my parents in Melbourne. I guess it was a safety precaution in case I did not come back. As part of an army family, Dad and Mum supported my going and just wished me good luck.

Jan was worried that our old Holden was not reliable and too big.

'What about a Mini? I'd be much happier with one,' she said.

'Sounds great,' I said. 'We'll pay it off with the tax-free money.'

'What will I live off?' Jan asked.

'I should only need a couple of dollars. I'll allot the rest to the bank back here.'

With a sense that everything was in order, on the night of 13 June 1966, Jan took me out to the base to get on the Boeing 707 that had been chartered to take us to Saigon.

HOMECOMING

At the end of 12 months (to the day) on active duty I returned home to Canberra. I was the last of the original group to return. A staggered change-over schedule had been established by sending us home at regular intervals starting early in the new year. This ensured that there were always enough experienced pilots to introduce reinforcements to operational flying procedures. Once again, my last-home position was 'jokingly' credited to my being the youngest.

I find it interesting that one thing I cannot recall is my trip home. I know that I met my wife at RAAF Fairbairn in Canberra, but what aircraft or how we proceeded from one place to another is a mystery. The whole concept of being home was surreal. I remember feelings of uneasiness, of incompleteness and a strange sense of being lost. While I loved the opportunity to be back with my wife and family, I wondered what I had achieved and who cared anyway.

It was like returning from a business trip. Wife meets you at the airport and everything is back to normal routine, no big deal. While you did not anticipate that everybody would be out there waving flags, it gradually becomes evident that the sacrifices had little meaning or credence in the lives of general society. But, for the individual, there was the rebuilding of a relationship with his wife and family. Children who wondered who this strange man was. In my case a three-year old who was too young to remember back a year. A wife who recognised changes in the man she knew and puzzled at the reasons why. I felt an overwhelming desire to hold them and be with them all the time.

I was given six weeks of leave to be with my family. We went to the snow as a contrast to my year of intense heat. We had lost a baby boy at birth just before I went away and were keen to have another child. Unfortunately, this boy was also to not survive his birth. It all seemed so soon that I reported to the squadron to do training with army units.

To my surprise I was posted to a flying instructors course at Sale in Victoria on my return. It was an unaccompanied posting, which did not please me much after having just been away for a year. Another six months of separation was not what I wished for.

Settling back into the routine was hard for me. I struggled with the artificial nature of the instructor's course where everything needed to be done 'by the book'. Instructing routines had to be learned verbatim and there was no room for adaptation to the circumstances. I struggled to apply myself, drank a bit, and talked at length to my wife on the telephone. I could do the work, wanted to help others learn as a natural instinct, but could not overcome a defiant attitude and restless spirit.

The chief instructor recognised that I could teach after taking me for an instructional flight to evaluate my instructional ability, but was concerned because I did not do it the same way as everyone else. He argued that it would confuse the students if they were told different things by different teachers. Little did I know at that time that I was about to spend my life proving that I was right and, in fact, this was essential if we were to meet the needs of individual students. This included achieving a Doctor of Education in student learning. But back to the story, I was suspended from the course because he did not feel I would conform, and probably more to the point, because I would not say that I would toe the line.

When asked by the Chief Flying Instructor whether they should take a risk on me, I responded that that was his job and he needed to make up his own mind. He did that immediately saying that I left him little choice. In a few short flippant and irrational words I had destroyed a traditional future through which I could have advanced my career.

I was actually devastated when the axe fell and cried for ages on the phone with my wife. I knew I wanted to teach and was devastated that they could not recognise the quality of my teaching. My friends on the course tried to get me to meet with the authorities and ask for another chance. But I could not bring myself to back-track. I told the commanding officer that they were making a huge mistake as they were sacking an outstanding teacher, which was how I felt inside.

I was put into limbo, still at Sale separated from my wife, while a decision was made about my future. Some luck came my way in that my ex-rugby coach at the RAAF Academy happened to be Director of Postings and doing a refresher course at Sale at the time, before he went to Butterworth in Malaysia as a fighter pilot. He recognised my situation after his experience in Korea and felt that I should be given a break, sending me and my family to Butterworth also. I really appreciated his understanding and support. At the time I was happy to accept second prize and head overseas with my wife. A posting to Malaysia was a jewel in an air force career, providing excitement, difference and improved financial rewards.

'The digger's best friend', Canberra Times, 7 September 1966.

CHAPTER 3

ORIENTATION TO PHUOC TUY PROVINCE

June to July 1966

We arrived in Saigon on the morning of 14 June 1966. The 707 disgorged us on to the tarmac in the northern corner of Tan Son Nhut Airport. No international passenger terminals for us. We looked around in awe.

There were planes everywhere. Both in the sky and on the ground. Watching the long line of planes on final I could see that the next plane was landing before the last one was off the runway. There seemed to be several planes on the other runway taking off one behind the other. There was certainly no room for a mistake. Then there were helicopters coming and going in all directions, seemingly without control. In the background I could hear the sounds of bombing and artillery fire.

'Where's that?' someone asked.

'In those hills over there to the west,' I replied. You could see the puffs of smoke where the bombs and shells were landing.

Just then two F100s went speeding past as they scrambled on an emergency response. The taxiway was banked so that they could travel at high speed and reduce time to take off.

'Shit, I wouldn't want to get in their road,' said Geoff.

'What happens to aircraft landing when they charge out like that?'

'There are two runways, one for take-off and one for landing. They just cut in front of the next one in line to take off,' said our Air Transport Office (ATO) guide.

'I have never seen so many aircraft.' There was no doubt we were in a war zone.

'Over this way,' our ATO guide called. 'There are three "Baby Hercs" (Lockheed C123 Light Transports) to take you to Vung Tau.'

'Where are our Caribous?' Geoff asked.

'You mean Wallaby Airlines? They do a regular courier run around Vietnam and are not available,' he answered.

'How long will it take?'

'Only about 20 minutes, depending a bit on traffic.'

We filed into the back of the C123. It was pretty dirty and obviously well used. There were rows of canvas seats along the sides and we packed in side by side. Then the back door was rising, the engines cranked over and we were moving, seemingly without any fuss. We joined the queue for take-off. There looked to be about 15 aircraft in front of us. But, it didn't take long for us to be at the head of the queue and rolling down the runway. The C123 clanked and rumbled as she built up speed. As the wheels came up we went into a steep bank, obviously getting out of the next plane's way. Two more F100s flashed by.

We only climbed to a couple of thousand feet and bounced along in the turbulence. We skirted Saigon and flew down across a big river; lots of mangrove swamp and out over the sea. There was a small mountain range out to the left. Down in the bay there were many ships at anchor. We passed around a small peninsula and started to descend into Vung Tau.

I could see the sea out each side, but not our landing area. Suddenly we 'crashed' into the ground with a loud rattle of metal reinforcement. Reverse was applied and the aircraft came to a quick halt. As it wheeled off to the side of the runway I could see that it was an old and short strip with sheets of metal reinforcing at each end. There were mainly small observation type aircraft and helicopters parked in bays with reinforcing and sand bag walls. There were a couple of hangers and lots of tents. It was very reminiscent of what we saw in World War II movies.

Without the engines stopping, the back door lowered and we trundled out. Our engineering officer was there to guide us to our ops (operations) tent. The C123 quickly lumbered away and did a quick and steep take-off. The other two aircraft followed in close order.

In the ops tent we met up with the CO (commanding officer), who had arrived before us with an advanced party. We also met up with the pilots who had come across from our helicopter support flight in Butterworth, Malaysia. One was Frank, who I had known at Richmond before I transferred to helicopters. He was a loud, wild man with a receding hairline and a big nose. This nose often led him into trouble. He enjoyed his drink and could con anybody. He and I were to have several interesting experiences together over the next year.

It was bloody hot inside the tent.

'Well, welcome, guys, to the warm Vung Tau, the Riviera of the East,' the boss started. 'Don't be fooled by the apparent quiet and friendliness of the village. It's a VC [Viet Cong] rest area and most people have divided loyalties. You need to be on guard at all times and very careful about where and when you go downtown. This is no jolly; people die in town most nights.'

Everyone looked from one another with a bit of a shocked look. After all, weren't we in control of our base? No-one asked any questions.

He outlined that we were on show in working with the army, a difficult relationship. We needed to develop tactics quickly and effectively. We could not follow the pattern of the US helicopters as we did not have enough. However, he was happier doing small scale, quick and incisive operations anyway. Remember you are the captain of the aircraft and have final say on what it gets to do, he stressed.

The boss handed over to the intel (intelligence) officer and he gave us a briefing on the enemy activity in the province, their strengths and normal base camp areas. He warned us that they were a highly mobile force that could strike anywhere in the province at any time.

'Always be on guard, both in the air and on the ground,' he warned. 'Fly only at treetop level, or below. Or transit at a height above small arms range, about 2000 feet (615 metres). In between is asking for trouble. On the ground, never wander far from your helicopter. Always carry your firearms. Thanks, guys, have a safe tour. I will see you every morning with the latest update.'

We were then handed over to the armourer who had a truck full of weapons outside. We were each issued with a 9mm Browning automatic pistol. We were put through a refresher of how to strip, clean and generally look after our weapon. Some chose to also have a rifle. Most of these were returned after a short while as they were cumbersome to lug around, were heavy and were regarded as more trouble than they were worth. After all, we were not there to engage in man-to-man fighting with the enemy but to carry others who were much better at that than us.

It was early afternoon and we were taken into town by truck to settle into our accommodation and have a feed. Most of us had been to Asia before and the trip into town looked like any other trip from the airport to town. It was a single lane dirt road with deep monie drains (monsoon ditches) along the side to take away the rain water and to carry irrigation water for the rice fields, which were all along the roadside. Traffic along the road was pedestrians of all size and shape, bicycles loaded with all manner of goods, a few motorcycles carrying far too many passengers and the odd 'odd' three-wheel tractor. There were no civilian cars, just military vehicles.

'Iroquois join Caribou in Vietnam', RAAF News, July 1966.

Houses were all just shanties. The most significant difference was the use of flattened soft drink cans to form shingles. It was the dry season, so the yards were swept dirt, with the odd pig wallowing in a wet spot. The raised dykes around the paddy fields were the tracks linking each little group of huts.

The women, especially teenage girls, were the only ones that were distinctively dressed. They wore an ousai, which, if they were school age, was long black silken pants with a white three-quarter over blouse with long sleeves, split down the sides and buttoned to the neck. They wore a woven rice straw hat in the shape of a cone. Older women had a wider range of coloured tops, but normally black pants.

Very occasionally there was a man in black pyjamas, which made us wonder whether he was a VC as this was their traditional uniform. But generally men wore a pair of shorts or pants and a shirt, Western style.

As we approached the outskirts of the village itself the buildings started to become more substantial. They were in the French style, square-shaped with white rendered walls and red-tiled rooves. Most were two storeys and fairly run down. The roads became bitumen streets. We passed along the edge of town and up to the foreshore. There was a low stone wall along the sea side of the street with a stony beach beyond. But all the houses along this street were the most substantial that we could see and in better repair.

We stopped outside one with the name Villa Anna. This was to be our home away from home and our retreat at night. It had a wall of nearly

2 metres around it, substantial grounds with a few large fig trees and several outhouses. There was a guard on the large wrought iron gates at the rear of the premises, which was the main entrance. It looked pretty good at first glance; certainly better than living in a tent.

Just along the foreshore in the adjoining block was another similar villa. This was where the other ranks were to live and where the kitchen was located. There already had been some development on this site with several tin sheds assembled within the grounds to provide a mess hall/boozer and more accommodation.

'There's a meal waiting for you down the road,' Stan said. He was the equipment officer and had arrived with the advance party.

'Look at all the ships parked off the coast; what's the go?'

'They're waiting their turn to go up the river to Saigon,' Stan informed me.

'Not too much sand on the beach. All those pebbles make it look like England.'

We turned into the villa to get our first meal in Vietnam.

When we arrived back at Villa Anna we realised it was not going to be all that sweet. There were six to eight hessian fold-up stretchers in each room, leaving the minimum space to move around in. Our room was for the young guns, no-one over 30: Bruce, the polished professional; Cliff, a laconic guy; Ted, a quiet Pom; Stan the serious one; and me. We moved in, with a bed saved for Dave, the joker. Dave's wife was to give birth in our first week on tour and he had been given leave to arrive a week later.

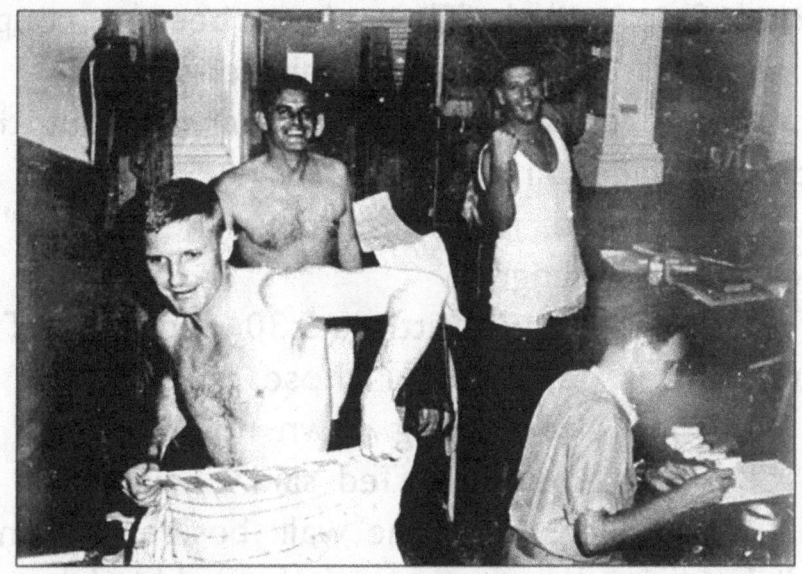

Our sleeping quarters Cliff, Ted, Stan and myself.

'This is a bit cosy,' Cliff said with a smile.
'I bags the corner over here,' I said.
'This'll do me,' Bruce said.
'I guess I go here,' Ted followed. Stan already had his set-up in the middle.

I made my bed and set up the mosquito net. Then I arranged my gear as best I could under the bed and decided it was time to do my daily weapon check. This involved cleaning and checking the pistol.

'What was it that armourer said about sliding the action forward?'

'Make sure you use an empty magazine,' Bruce responded.

'Let's not have a bullet flying around this room,' Stan added. 'There have been a couple of near misses down in the airmen's area.'

Would we get through a year without this type of accidental discharge?

'What time is the evening meal, Stan?' I asked, always hungry.

'They have two sittings-5.30 and 6.30. The latter one is designed for those on duty.'

'Anyone else coming down now?'

'I'm with you, Bob,' Ted said.

We strolled down the walk beside the small wall between the street and the pebbled beach. There was a continuous stream of Vietnamese walking along the footpath. Something you became accustomed to was seeing individuals just prop along the wall and urinate-or worse-and move on again, both men and women. It was important to watch where you put your feet. Out over the bay the sun was low in the sky over the ships.

'Feel like a beer before tea?'

'Sure,' Ted said.

After dinner I was starting to feel pretty tired so I strolled back and went to bed. I slept soundly till the gunfire outside the villa.

We had been briefed not to rush outside, as that was often what the disturbance was designed to do. An antipersonnel mine would be discharged outside the door. We were told to arm ourselves and wait for further orders; let the guards do their job. So we lay there, pistols in hand. Wondering what was happening. Nobody spoke.

Then a guard appeared at the door and said all was well. Something had moved at the front of the villa and the guard had fired a warning shot.

'Shit! What would we do if some VC came over the fence?'

'Good question. I didn't feel too good just lying here,' said Cliff.

'Maybe we had better talk about a plan of action tomorrow,' said Bruce.

With that we started to drift back to sleep. My thoughts were that the guard is obviously awake, so I can afford to sleep. Others talked the next day about remaining awake for the rest of the night, disturbed by the thought of the enemy infiltrating our quarters. But I was lucky; I could sleep anywhere.

The next day, 15 June, a crew were tasked to do a courier run up to the Australian Task Force location at Nui Dat. I went with a group down to the rifle range to practise firing our pistols. This is something I did more than most. I enjoyed shooting and aimed to be a marksman with my pistol so that if I ever needed to use it, I wouldn't miss.

There was also some equipment to unpack out on the flight line. We went out to help there in the afternoon. It was interesting to watch the different types of aircraft take off and land. Many we had never seen in Australia. The majority were called close air support aircraft and had short take-off and landing capability, plus were highly manoeuvrable. Under the wings they had a range of rockets and some had machine guns. The way the pilots threw them around they were obviously fun things to fly.

Before leaving I saw that I was tasked to fly first thing in the morning with Cliff on a courier run to the Task Force.

The second night passed without incident. We had arranged who would watch which entrance to our room. We wouldn't fire unless we were absolutely sure it was the enemy. It was hot in the villa and we all slept on top of our bedding.

For most tasks we were woken before dawn. The guards had the task of coming in quietly and waking you up, obviously hoping they did not startle you and create an attack incident. In a war zone it was usually assumed that the negative had happened as everyone was on edge and someone touching you could cause a violent, life-threatening reaction. I did not envy the guards their task. You either got up and went for a sound meal before roughing the rest of the day, or grabbed another few minutes in bed. The meals served by the air force cooks were far superior to those available at army messes, or, worse still, hard rations. However, we all became quite good at 'modifying' the various tins of food in the ration pack to create some culinary delights-relatively speaking.

I rose and went to breakfast before jumping in a jeep to drive out to the flight line. There was Cliff and I plus another crew. It only took ten minutes to drive out there at a leisurely pace.

We fronted for an intelligence briefing.

'There have only been fleeting sightings of VC groups to the east of Nui Dat,' the intell officer told us and pointed to the map. 'Out past Long Phuoc and Long Tan. But, be warned, they are from a well-organised battalion of local guerrillas called D445. It's important that you anticipate they could be anywhere, anytime. Be cautious, be prepared.'

We were issued with a flak vest and an armoured breastplate. The armour was made of plastic, but still fairly heavy. We wore the flak vest to catch any bullet fragments that occurred after a bullet hit the breastplate. Together they were cumbersome and made you very hot. But there was no hesitancy in wearing them. Later we were to also get steel-armoured seats for the helicopters. They provided protection underneath, at the back and sides. The entrance side plate slid back and forth. We were then like Ned Kelly, with only our legs exposed.

I went over to the helicopter and did a pre-flight check. Cliff went and signed the maintenance release. We had a couple of parcels, a bag of mail, a soldier and an officer to take with us. We cranked up and took off to the north east.

Vung Tau was on a small peninsula of land, 3 kilometres wide and 15 kilometres long, which jutted out into the South China Sea. A single road wound its way north-east to the provincial capital, Ba Ria, through the mangrove swamps. We climbed to 2000 feet and flew just east of the road. There was a large range of hills (Long Hai) to our east at the end of a sweeping half-moon bay, about 10 kilometres away.

After about five minutes we had crossed the mangroves and approached rice paddies, then rubber plantations. We passed to the east of Ba Ria between two populated areas, picking up a road that went out to the north. Five kilometres up this road was the Task Force area. It was in a rubber plantation and alongside a small hill called Nui Dat. The Task Force took this name for its location. Later, we came to realise that all small hills in Vietnam were called Nui Dat.

The area to the north was a sea of jungle with the occasional rubber plantation. To the west were two ranges of hills (Nui Dinh, Nui Thi Vai) 6 to 10 kilometres away. This was the topography of the area in which we were to operate for the next year.

Cliff landed on the helicopter pad and a digger arrived in a jeep to collect the gear and the passengers.

'Stay with the chopper,' said Cliff. 'I'll check with operations on what they want us to do next.'

He disappeared up a path through the rubber trees in the direction of some tents. There was a lot of activity with diggers digging trenches, laying out wire and moving stores. We had noticed the artillery positioned on the south side of the area, but had not seen any sign of battalion troop placements. We later learned that they were to the north and east of the position. It was hot and dry, so we broke out some water to drink.

Cliff arrived back after 15 minutes and said we just had to go home to Vung Tau. We followed the same route back. As we passed over the sea the door gunners did some test firing of their M60 machine guns. They hung from a strap attached to the roof of the helicopter which meant the machine gun would dangerously swivel around. Luckily, we were quickly able to get fixed mountings from US stores that allowed a lot more control. Most importantly, they provided fixed arcs of fire so the guns could not be inadvertently fired into the helicopter. After a total of 25 minutes flying time I had completed my first operational sortie.

Tasking was slow at this time. I did not fly again for five days. That was only to do some test firing with the new M60 mounts. My next operational task was not until two days later on 23 June.

All of our time in Vietnam was not 'on duty' or more simply 'at war'. In two ways this is not completely accurate. If there was any sort of emergency or major attack, such as the Battle of Long Tan, then everyone was instantly called to operations and was on duty. Similarly, we were living in a war zone and although the town of Vung Tau was often like a beach resort, one had to always be prepared for the unexpected or some form of action by a VC sympathiser against us. This often took the form of a hand grenade rolled into a bar or shop where Western military were present. A yell of 'grenade' had people diving for cover everywhere with drinks flying into the air plus people pushing and shoving each other as they tried to get under the bar or table.

Occasionally someone was shot by a sniper just walking around the streets. Quite amazingly, Vung Tau was also the rest area for the VC and so we needed to always be aware that anybody could be less than sympathetic to our presence. As is the way of guerrilla warfare, many Vietnamese changed occupations between day and night; say, a shopkeeper by day and a soldier by night. This applied to men, women and even children. One was always aware of a young person showing too much attention to you or your things in case they sent you home with an unpleasant surprise.

However, we still chose to explore the town of Vung Tau and the surrounding general area. It was a small town and typical of Asia. Shops were small family-operated concerns at the front of the home. Each and every one had its own character and seemingly a capacity to do anything.

Bargaining was the normal process of transaction and anything they did not have they could get for you. In this early stage of our arrival in town there was very limited merchandise that we wanted. This rapidly changed as they determined what we would buy and got supplies from somewhere.

There was an area of town in which there were bars and the associated bar girls. While many frequented these places, after the first time a grenade was rolled into one while I was having a drink, I rarely visited them. The stories of what could happen to you in these places kept this boy well away.

I was much happier to visit the American Officers' Club. It had a wider range of entertainment, better food, cheap drinks and, I must admit, more conducive company. It was also only two blocks from our Villa Anna.

Similarly, the BX (American Base Exchange) was a large department store where you could buy almost everything. Bottles of spirits were only $1. LPs (long playing records) were similarly often only $1. I bought a portable stereo record player and headphones plus several LPs for $40. This became my prime source of relaxation during the many hours spent waiting for the next job. My record collection just grew and grew.

On one of these days we went to the back beach. It was a long sandy beach with a few waves. Over the next few months an Australian club was built here and it became a central focus for people on 'in-country' R&R (rest and recuperation). We also drove up onto the western headland to have a look at the outlook. There were several very large houses in this area that belonged to very wealthy plantation owners or Saigon merchants and were their 'beach' houses.

Bruce, Cliff and I decided to have a meal in the American Officers' Club.

'Let's go to the bar for a drink first.'

'What'll you have?' asked the bartender.

'What sort of beer do you have?'

'Bud, Millers and Coors.'

'Three Buds, thanks.'

'This stuff is so watery.'

'Refreshing enough,' Bruce responded.

As we sat enjoying our drink the bar started to fill up. Many pilots arrived in their flying suits. It was obviously the end of the day's missions. The noise level started to grow. We noticed a particularly loud group in the corner. Then we saw that Frank was in the centre of the group. Good old Frank, telling stories again. He had an air force-wide reputation as a larrikin. We were to fly together a few weeks later in the Battle of Long Tan.

He saw us and wandered over.

'G'day,' he said. 'Just organised an Ml rifle in exchange for a slouch hat. What are you up to?'

'Just having a drink, mate,' I replied. 'Thought we might have a meal. Do you know what they are like?'

'Usual American stuff. Hamburgers, chicken or processed beef. Cheap enough. The place swings a bit later though. Worth hanging around.'

'Thanks. Want a drink?' I responded.

'Sure, got time for one,' Frank said, never one to pass up a drink. 'I have to go and see the equipo (equipment officer) about a hat.'

We were enjoying our drink when an American pilot arrived with a beer for Frank.

'Thanks, mate. This is Hank; he flies Broncos. Organised a trip with him one day if the boss OKs it. This is Bruce, Cliff, Bob,' Frank said.

'Hi, guys. Great mate you've got here. How's it been for you?' Hank asked.

'We haven't seen much action yet,' I said. 'Only been here a couple of weeks. How long have you been here?'

'This is my tenth month. I'm on short time. Looking forward to heading back to the old US of A.'

'What do we have to look forward to?' Bruce asked.

'It's not a bad province,' Hank replied. 'The activity is all pretty small-scale stuff. Almost no anti-aircraft to worry about. Not like up north. I have taken a few small arms hits. But that's all. We give 'em hell if they shoot back. Tends to turn them off.'

'Sounds OK,' Bruce said.

'Got to go, guys. See you again sometime,' Hank said as he gestured to a departing group of pilots.

'I'm off home to change,' Frank said. 'Might see you around here later.'

'Your round, Frank,' I quipped.

'Buy it later,' he responded as he headed off.

'I'm hungry; let's get a feed,' Cliff said.

We sat down to a table and looked at the menu. It was bistro style, with a few displays of salads, bread and dessert. You ordered your main choice at the servery.

'I guess I'll try the hamburger with chips.'

'I'm trying the chicken,' Bruce said.

'Well, I'll try the steak and then we can see what's on offer,' Cliff said.

We got a salad and some bread while we were waiting. The meals came quickly, so we guessed they were already cooked out the back. Typical fast food approach.

'At least the hamburger's a big one.'

'The chicken's OK,' Bruce added.

'Well, the steak's tasteless,' Cliff said. 'I prefer the meat back in our mess.'

After trying some of their gelatinous desserts we moved back to the bar area.

A band was warming up and there was a crowd growing, including some nurses and Red Cross girls.

'The scenery is better down here.'

'But there's ten to one,' Cliff remarked.

'I see Frank's doing OK, as usual,' Bruce said as he pointed over to the corner.

'It's amazing how he can always be in the thick of the action.'

We had a few drinks, listened to the music and talked to a couple of US pilots. It was approaching curfew and we decided we should walk the couple of blocks back to Villa Anna. During the year we went to the American mess about once a week for a change, but not for the food.

On non-flying days we were also rostered to be the duty officer. This involved spending the day out at the airfield, usually in the operations area. The duty officer organised crews to and from their helicopter and Villa Anna.

Occasionally we also did live firing training with our pistols and other weapons. It wasn't all go, go, go—there were lengthy periods of wait, wait, wait.

Once we moved away from Vung Tau and were in the grip of army tasking we spent a lot of time waiting for our next order. More often than not we needed to stay in the vicinity of our helicopter, not that we had too much desire to wander around as our helicopter was the quickest way out of trouble if any arose. In an average 12-hour day we would fly for up to five hours doing 30 to 40 take-offs and landings (sorties) and consequently sat around for at least seven hours.

My next operational task was with Bruce and we again flew to Nui Dat with a small load of parcels and personnel. Then we took the Task Force Commander, Brigadier Jackson, on a reconnaissance visit to Long Phuoc, where Operation Enoggera was being carried out. Our briefing had been that we were careful about operating into insecure landing areas. This looked very close to the action as there were fires and obvious troop movements on the ground.

'Is this pad secure?' Bruce asked.

'Anywhere a brigadier goes is secure,' he retorted.

We landed and he disappeared into the surrounding jungle. The sight of all the soldiers around the pad lying with their rifles pointing outwards did not give us any comfort. We remained in the helicopter, with it 'cocked' ready to take off very quickly.

Sure enough, a fire-fight broke out close to the clearing. We believed that the enemy were after our helicopter, so we started the engines. We looked around for the brigadier.

'Can anybody see some movement in our direction?' Bruce asked.

'No. Just people ducking for cover,' I responded.

'Let's get out of here,' Bruce said as he pulled pitch and we rose out of the jungle.

'Albatross, this is sunray, get back here.'

'Sunray, request that the area be secured.'

'Albatross, contact broken off, return immediately.'

'Sunray, has the pad been secured?'

We bantered for a while. Mainly to let some time pass before we went back in. The brigadier was fuming.

'What the hell did you guys come up here for if you're frightened of the odd gunshot?' he retorted. 'You guys chicken or something? You do as I say and whatever I ask.'

We chose not to continue the discussion. The CO did, however, the next day after our report. He pointed out to Brigadier Jackson that the pilot had sole responsibility for his helicopter and would use it in an appropriate manner.

This episode became a thorn in the side of relationships between the army and the air force for quite some time. We operated our helicopters according to sound use of air power and under air force command, whereas the brigadier wanted us to be at his command and used as trucks. We always met the demands of his tasking, but not always in the manner in which he wanted us to do it.

After we dropped him off we returned to Vung Tau. Our trip had taken 1 hour and 20 minutes. I was then crewed with Frank to do troop positioning that afternoon. We did three lifts with replacement troops to Long Phuoc from Nui Dat, a distance of 3 kilometres. We then returned home with a total of one hour's flying time.

It had been an eventful day. It introduced me to the sounds and sights of battle.

Others had more eventful engagements with the enemy. Bruce and Cliff had landed in a small clearing to pick up some troops when they came under fire from a sniper up in a tree. Return fire by the door gunners silenced his efforts and the helicopter withdrew without damage. Laddie, our flight commander, who was a veteran fighter pilot from World War II, was responding to a call to do a medical evacuation from a small fortified village when he came under fire on approach. The door gunners fired into the area and Laddie continued his approach. The injured, a small girl, was safely taken to hospital, without damage to the helicopter once again. These occurrences helped us realise that the enemy could be anywhere, but that it was also difficult for him to hit the helicopter and cause damage. We were not just 'sitting ducks' as some felt.

The next day I flew with Laddie to Nui Dat to collect an army intelligence officer who we took to Saigon and then to Ben Hoa-15 kilometres to the northeast of Saigon and about 60 kilometres from Nui Dat-for briefings. While at Ben Hoa we watched as an engagement with the enemy took place on the airfield boundary. There was artillery fire from airfield defences and bombing by US aircraft, with the occasional salvo of mortars from the VC in return. We were to learn that many of these mortars that the VC fired were carried down from North Vietnam by individuals over a mountainous track called the Ho Chi Minh trail. Once expended, the soldier had to trek back to get more supplies.

'Baptism of fire for Iroquois', RAAF News, August 1966.

'Do we have to worry about that fire-fight over there?' I asked an American ground crew.

'Nah, they haven't got anything that can reach this far,' he replied.

'What about those buildings over there?' I asked, pointing to some damaged buildings 100 metres away.

'Oh, those,' he said. 'They were hit the night before last. When Charlie crept up close, inside the wire, and let off a few mortars.'

I was glad we would not be staying overnight.

In the afternoon, we flew back to Saigon and then to Nui Dat and home.

To give a perspective of the size of the province we were operating within, this trip took us across and out of Phuoc Tuy Province with a total flying time of less than two hours. So, anywhere in the province was less than an hour flying time away.

When we got home in the evening our topic of conversation over a few drinks was the incredible activity that was happening at these two massive air bases. We were astounded at the number of aircraft in the air. As well, the close proximity of attacks by bomber aircraft to the airfield perimeter highlighted the difference to our quiet province.

***

Dave had arrived after the birth of his first daughter. He settled into his bunk and joined us in the afternoon as we cleaned our weapons. Suddenly there was an almighty bang. A bullet went flying around the room. There was no time to duck or do anything.

'Holy shit!' was the retort.

Dave was sitting looking down at his gun. We were looking at the marks on the wall where the bullet had gone. Luckily, he had the barrel pointing upwards. There were three ricochet marks.

'What happened?' Dave asked.

'Were there bullets in the magazine?' Bruce asked.

'Yep. What else would there be?' Dave said.

'Well, it has to be empty. Don't you remember the warning?'

'What warning? Nobody showed me what to do when they gave me the pistol today.'

'Well, let's go and have a beer on the fact nobody got shot. And, also to wet the baby's head,' Cliff suggested.

'You won't do that again, will you, you dipstick?'

Our fear had been realised. Luckily, no-one was hurt. It did not happen again in our room.

The next day I flew with Ted up to Nui Dat. Our task was to take one of the COs on a reconnaissance into the north-west corner of the province. He needed to see the lay of the land as he prepared for a major clearing exercise. Enemy activity had been reported in the area. A search of a village was also to be conducted. The area was mainly jungle with a little cultivation around the village. The Nui Nghe range of hills was in the western section of the area. We flew at 2000 feet, which put us up out of harm's way and gave him a good view of the topography. Everything looked so innocuous from this lofty perspective.

I was home inside two hours and did not fly again for three days. However, I got to be busier on the next flying day, at last. A new role for at least one helicopter had been designated Kangaroo Courier or Standby. The helicopter pad at Nui Dat was now called Kangaroo Pad. A helicopter positioned at Kangaroo Pad on standby could be likened to a taxi, sitting around waiting for a 'fare' and not knowing where it would take you.

We always ensured that we had a good briefing of the intelligence situation before we left Vung Tau so that we understood where enemy activity had been reported and which areas were more or less secure for our operations. We then updated this with a further briefing from the operations tent at Nui Dat, which outlined overnight activity by Task Force groups. Our brief was to operate in and out of relatively secure locations, and the army often had a different perspective of what was 'secure'. It also became apparent that we were able to get a much broader intelligence brief in Vung

Tau than the information that was disseminated at Task Force.

This helicopter was basically at the beck and call of the brigadier. It arrived at Nui Dat in the early morning and left in the evening, doing anything that it was asked to do during the day. I always felt that this role had originated out of a compromise with the brigadier over the time Bruce and I left him stranded.

On my first Kangaroo Courier we got to fly for four and a half hours and did 23 sorties. We took people to and from forward element positions and down to Vung Tau. We flew a meal of fresh food out to the forward elements in thermal containers. We evacuated a sick soldier back to the medical area. We hauled captured rice back to the Task Force area. It was very routine stuff, but busy and important. Fortunately, this was indicative of what lay ahead, and we were to become even busier.

The next day was 30 June and I flew a C&C (command and control) mission with Ted. The squadron had acquired a set of command radios that could be installed in the back of the helicopter. A command team could then sit in the back of the helicopter and have radio contact with elements on the ground. It was always interesting watching three leaders, each on a different radio frequency, trying to communicate with each other over the noise of the helicopter, while also communicating with the ground. It allowed them to be very flexible – and safe – in their location as they overviewed an operation. In this case it was what was called a road runner operation. It was a clearing patrol along the highway to Saigon and the brigadier wished to see what was happening and remain in contact with his other elements.

Our first month had ended and we were fairly frustrated by the lack of activity. Flying had been limited. We felt it may have been a problem with the lack of interaction between the army and air force on the ways to use helicopters. They seemed to prefer to walk or travel in APCs (armoured personnel carriers). Slowly but surely this changed.

I wrote a letter home each day. Separation was difficult when you weren't busy. Mail from Australia was often sporadic, so we would get several letters at once from home. I always put them in order and read them all at once. Others saved them for one a day. Writing so frequently meant there was often little to talk about, but just reading about the routine things that were happening each day or the small achievements of your child was wonderful. Life was lots of routine boredom dispersed with moments of terror in an environment of isolation from the 'normal' world. We sat around drinking and talking of an evening to while away the time. For many, alcohol became the sedative of choice.

July was a busier month. I flew on 20 out of the 31 days. On the first I was tasked with Laddie to be Kangaroo Courier. This was to be one of ten times that I fulfilled this role during July. The jobs we were given to do were usually very routine: take someone from one command position to another and return for briefings. Collect an injured or sick person and return him to the Aid Post. On one occasion we collected two wounded VC and took them for medical aid. They were under guard, of course.

To provide a break from hard rations we would be tasked to take a hot meal out to a forward position. For instance, I recall carrying steak and vegetables to the front line with diggers dropping back to our clearing, having a meal and then returning to their posts facing the enemy. Ice-cream was another favourite. When you relate these experiences to World War II diggers they feel these troops had it too good, certainly compared to the hardships they endured through poor and extended supply lines, not to mention attacks by the enemy on these lines.

Perhaps one of the most outstanding trips was carrying hot bread. We arrived at the briefing for Kangaroo Standby at our ops room.

After discussion about the latest intelligence information we spoke to Laddie about our tasking.

'You have to go to back beach and pick up a load on your way up,' Laddie informed us.

'What is it?'

'Don't know.'

'OK. Let's go,' I said to Dave.

We flew the two minutes across to ALSG (Australian Logistic Support Group) at back beach. A truck was waiting. Once we had closed down they started to load large plastic bags into the back of the helicopter. They were full of hot bread. They loaded the back till it was chock a block.

On the way up to Nui Dat the helicopter was full of the enticing aroma of fresh bread.

'Do you think they would notice if we ate one, boss?' asked Bluey from the back.

'Sounds like a good idea,' I replied. He slipped a loaf out of one bag and broke it into four bits for us to 'sample'.

'There's nothing like hot, fresh bread.'

The next day Laddie and I were tasked to support 6RAR in the final stages of Operation Enoggera in Long Phuoc. This included carrying captured weapons and rice the 2 kilometres back to the Task Force. So, although we did 13 sorties, we only flew for a total of one and a half hours.

Then the next day Ted and I took some of this rice to a small village, Duc Than. This was part of the support we were providing after a search and destroy mission by 5RAR just to the north when they were looking for VC. It was obvious that the villagers were undernourished and short of food. This offering was a part of our building of relationships within the province.

In the afternoon we did a trip with an intelligence officer out to the area of Long Tan village and on to Saigon then Ben Hoa and back. Once again it was a real experience to mingle with so many aircraft in such a busy area.

The next day Max and I did two trips to the north of the Province. Max was one of the pilots from Butterworth; he was quiet, tall, sandy haired with a moustache A no-nonsense sort of guy. He was later to earn a DFC (Distinguished Flying Cross) for a most courageous rescue of a SAS patrol. We flew up to Long Binh and collected an ARVN (Army of the Republic of Vietnam) officer and brought him to Vung Tau. Later in the day we returned him to Long Binh. This was an old French fort, now occupied by an ARVN group. I am sure he had an important briefing to attend. But he also managed to get some time downtown.

On 13 July, Cliff and I did resupply support for 5RAR. They were still involved in Operation Sydney, clearing the area around Binh Ba. It involved some hot meals again, plus the exchange of several diggers.

Two days later 5RAR initiated the second phase of Operation Sydney. Frank and I flew a C&C helicopter for the CO to oversee the operation, which involved two companies carrying out sweeps from opposite sides into two blocking companies. I then had a day off before doing a couple of more days on Kangaroo Courier. I decided to go down to the BX again and see what bargains were available. I bought a couple of LPs, one of which was an Eydie Gorme collection of hits. She became my singer of choice and I ended up with several of her LPs. I used to put one on the record player, put on my headphones and drift off into another world.

But my big buy was a slot car set. On the bargain stand was a 1/72nd scale set, including two build-yourself cars. I could see these in the shed out the back of Villa Anna and some entertaining nights racing each other. We bought more track over the year and several guys bought their own cars to assemble and race. We had some intense sessions on that track as competition became very fierce. Several guys became very adept at sliding the tail of their car out on the corner and sending the opponent flying off the track.

On the 20th, Max and I were flying to Xuan Loc, a major centre just north of Phuoc Tuy Province and East of Saigon. It was 40 kilometres due north on Route 2, which ran by the Task Force area. The weather closed in on us and we had to turn around. As we did this we recognised that there was a VC ambush established beside the road. A few shots were fired at us, but we were quickly out of range. We reported it to HQ (headquarters) and an artillery mission was carried out on the coordinates. The difference in firepower between the two sides was enormous. Any time the VC were discovered they were attacked with artillery or air power and had to retreat, quickly disappearing into the jungle. The essential key to their offensive was to get within attacking distance of the enemy without being detected.

When we got back to Nui Dat I did my first SAS (Special Air Service Squadron) insertion. One of our major roles in Vietnam was working with the SAS. It was necessary to develop new tactics for these operations, as we neither had the resources of the United States Forces nor the desire to copy their way of operating. The US used seven-man patrols, where we only used four men on patrol. This enabled us to lift the patrol and their equipment in one Bravo Model of our Iroquois helicopters. The Bravo had a smaller rotor width and lifting capacity than the larger models available to the US troops. The second significant difference was that we could aim to place the patrol behind the enemy lines undetected by using fewer helicopters on the insertion.

The CO developed the tactic of a two-helicopter operation for insertions. One was a high-flying lead helicopter and provided guidance to a low flying one. This helicopter could fly in at treetop level, land and depart from a small jungle clearing, and be well out of the area as the patrol disappeared into the undergrowth. Any enemy on the ground may have heard the sound of a helicopter rotor, but it would be hard to get a direction of travel as the sound is broken up by the trees when the helicopter is flying at treetop level and it could be easily confused with the sound from the higher-flying helicopter. Secondly, the time on the ground was so short-a matter of seconds-that the VC may not even have realised that a patrol had been dropped off. We carried out these operations without any preparatory attacks on the position to again maintain the element of surprise.

When you're twisting and turning between the treetops as low as you can go it's often difficult to navigate accurately to a small clearing in the jungle. As it was critically important to fly as low as possible to avoid detection, the second higher helicopter provided the navigation to the clearing. Flying at height reduced the danger of it being hit by bullets from riflemen on the ground. It could also look like a helicopter flying from one location to another and therefore not attract much interest. With left and right turn directions, the lead pilot guided the low-level helicopter as he looked down on the panorama below. Practice enabled the lead pilot to call when the low-level helicopter should flare.

The flare involved pulling back on the cyclic pitch control lever and lowering the collective, causing the helicopter nose to come up in the air and creating a lot of drag, which slowed the helicopter down very rapidly, at the same time kicking the tail rotor pedals so that you spun 180 degrees and could land and were already pointing towards home. If it is well coordinated, as the pilot put his nose down again he would have the clearing directly underneath him. This tactic allowed the helicopter to be travelling at maximum speed for most of the journey and only have to slow down for a short time to offload his passengers. This reduced its chances of being hit by ground fire.

The high level of teamwork that was developed within the squadron allowed these tactics to be applied without an accident and to the complete satisfaction of the SAS Squadron, who could be landed closer to the enemy without fear of being ambushed. Despite all the practice it was still an adrenaline-pumping experience fraught with all sorts of dangers and potential for disaster.

On this day, enemy movements had been reported to the northwest, near the Nui Dinh mountain range. We placed a patrol into a small clearing at the foot of the hills. We knew we were going to land in a very hostile area. The process was very quick, only a matter of seconds on the ground. Even with the distraction of the helicopter above and the fact that the VC may not have recognised that a lower helicopter at treetop level had entered the area it was more nerve tingling than anything else we did, and I returned feeling quite drained.

Two days later Max and I went back as the low-level helicopter again and extracted the patrol. We used the same two helicopter procedure. The higher helicopter made contact with the SAS patrol and established their exact location. It then guided the lower helicopter into the pick-up area. They had completed their mission of observing the enemy position without being discovered. They reported a major enemy camp with considerable troop movement. The patrol had been within metres of the enemy and not fired a single shot. This became the routine for many more missions with the SAS. I flew another insertion and extraction before the end of the month. However, over the next year not all of these missions were so routine.

On return to Vung Tau I teamed up with Ted and we flew a C&C helicopter over a convoy coming from Ben Hoa down Route 15. It was a convoy carrying the last of the 1RAR stores from the first tour. It arrived at Nui Dat without incident.

I did my first medivac (medical evacuation) involving our troops on 25 July when 6RAR became engaged with the enemy during Operation Brisbane. We flew out to the back of Long Tan, where the casualties had been brought back to a rear position. They had been given first aid. There was considerable blood. The diggers were in obvious pain. We flew them directly to the hospital at the back beach of Vung Tau. This flight only took ten minutes and the troops were in a hospital within an hour of being wounded. Little did I realise that this location would be the scene for an even more dangerous mission within a few weeks.

The next day I flew with the CO as we repositioned troops for 6RAR after more troops were killed and wounded during the night. Several of these had been caused by a stray round from our own artillery. I flew three further days of logistic support, troop positioning and C&C in support of 6RAR on this Operation to end my flying for July. With a total of 47 hours, July represented an average of my monthly flying time over the next year.

BACK IN SOUTH-EAST ASIA

The best thing about being sent to Butterworth was that I was out of the system and back into a more operational environment where flying was according to the conditions and not the book. I was to return to flying 'Goonie Birds' or 'Daks' as we fondly called the old DC3. Our little Transport Support Flight (TSF) flew these aircraft, providing transport support to the Australian fighter squadron based at Butterworth. We also carried Australian ambassadors to each South-East Asian country on tours of Colombo Plan aid projects, and ferried any other VIPs who were touring Asia.

Our VIP aircraft was the one that flew the Queen around Australia on her visit; it had ten comfortable seats plus a galley for steward service. We also did parachute resupply to isolated villages in the highlands to help them resist communist insurgents. There were just three crews (six pilots and three navigators) plus a flight commander.

Interestingly, all the pilots except the flight commander had served in Vietnam. The other pilots had flown Caribous. We were a group apart from the rest of the RAAF detachment that consisted of an operational headquarters, a fighter squadron and a hospital. This hospital was a major staging post for wounded diggers from Vietnam.

We spent extended periods of time away from home on the ambassadorial and VIP tours. I remember trips to the north of Thailand where we were building the road between Thailand and Burma using engineers from the Snowy Mountains Scheme, and a trip throughout Indonesia as we took radio technicians who installed the air-radio network throughout the Indonesian islands, improving air safety.

We visited Laos and marvelled at the great arch on the main road that had been built with gun-towers to protect the winning side after a revolution and had used the concrete donated by the USA to extend the airfield runway in Vientiane; we visited Angkor Wat in Cambodia and recognised the suffering of the Cambodian people; and, on visits to Brunei we enjoyed the hospitality of the British expatriates working the offshore oil fields at their elaborate sports club and golf course.

One VIP trip involved Gough Whitlam and his wife when he was Leader of the Opposition, on a visit to South-East Asia. He was not our favourite passenger as he was supporting those who wanted a withdrawal from Vietnam. We found him aloof and arrogant. On one trip to Bangkok we were able to take our wives and show them the floating markets and temples, before the traffic snarls made movement difficult and pollution introduced the need to use face-masks. However, these trips provided me with an intimate look at these South-East Asian nations as they struggled to emerge in the late 1960s.

A lot of our work was in support of the fighter squadrons and so we flew regularly between Butterworth, Tengah and Changi on Singapore and Ubon in Thailand. On one memorable occasion I had a mirage engine and 17 tradies on board, with a fighter pilot as my co-pilot, and as we set heading at Tengah after climbing to 2000 feet the starboard engine would not increase power. After checking for icing conditions and other minor issues with the carburettor, I decided to turn around and go back to Tengah as there were lots of afternoon thunderstorms ahead. As I rolled on bank the left engine had a major bearing failure, making a terrible banging noise. I feathered the engine, but the feathering switch was not correctly set, so the propeller ran down towards the feather and then ran back up again, meaning I had to continually reset the feathering button. I had just changed to Singapore Air Radio and declared an emergency, but when the language barrier became obvious I transferred to Tengah Radar. They gave me a heading to steer, but it was through clouds. I had the airfield visual, so I told them to keep an eye on me and I would glide back to the strip without going through clouds. Luckily, the need to climb to 2000 feet before setting heading had given me additional height to that which I would have had on a direct climb out, and so we safely landed on the end of the strip. We rolled to a stop and the tractor towed us back into the lines.

I received a 'Good Show' Award from the British Air Safety Group and featured on the cover of their magazine. My 'knucklehead' copilot was flabbergasted at my arms going everywhere as my engine fitter loadmaster and I tried to resurrect the starboard engine and tried to keep the port engine feathered, all the time sinking back towards the ground.

It was not all good times. Wherever we travelled the captain and copilot ate different meals as we regularly suffered from an upset stomach due to the different standards of food preparation and the use of human faeces as fertiliser in the vegetable gardens. We needed to do this even at the banquets that the ambassador frequently invited us to attend, where a wide range of 'interesting' dishes were presented. However, we enjoyed a very good stopover in the Bali Beach International Hotel when we took the crews who serviced the aircraft at Denpasar airfield during the changeover of the Sabres and Mirages, having to stay for 10 long days!

I found that I did not develop the empathy that so many have for developing countries today. While many suffered from abject poverty, greed and corruption was obviously rife amongst those we met on our missions. A distrust of local people was engendered in me from my Vietnam experience and I could not warm to those we saw on the streets. I had a clinical fascination with the social nuances and cultural symbols, which I feel was an inbuilt personal desire to understand people. But I led a very detached existence.

Luckily, there was not the same level of shameless exploitation of tourists or the over-development of beautiful locations-Phuket had no modern tourist facilities; Bali had one large multi-national hotel. Wherever we visited, the majority of tourists were local people enjoying their local heritage.

Our wives led pampered lives with servants to do the house cleaning and cooking. A close community was developed from the cultural isolation and our extended absence. Jan was carrying a baby when we arrived, but unfortunately, he did not survive following a premature birth. Our eldest daughter, Cathy, was born at the end of that year. Both she and our son, Brett, enjoyed the luxury of being pampered by servants. Having servants also allowed Jan and me to spend time together when I was home. We spent considerable time playing golf together. During the frequent times my family was at the base swimming pool I also coached children to play tennis.

Visiting Vietnam with TSF was most strange. When we carried the Australian Ambassador, we had a code status equal to the President of the USA that allowed us priority on take-off and landing over combat aircraft, so we would not be delayed in meeting ceremonial timelines. Those F100s had to wait for us. When we landed in small villages deep in enemy-controlled territory the war would appear to stop as the ambassador visited a hospital receiving Australian aid, or some other aspect of community infrastructure such as water supply, with a band accompanying him down the main thoroughfare. The pomp and ceremony seemed so out of place to those who had been shot at as they delivered war supplies on previous visits.

My most memorable trip was when we got permission to fly to Vung Tau on Christmas Day and bring out a group of seriously wounded diggers. Nurses from the evacuation hospital had suggested it and came along in an aircraft fitted out with canvas stretchers suspended from the ceiling and Christmas decorations. We served a Christmas dinner on the return trip. Although I missed some time with my small children it was a very heart-warming expedition and an outstanding Christmas present for a group of wounded diggers; six walking and eleven on stretchers.

'Vital Iroquois role in Viet battle', RAAF News, September 1966.

CHAPTER 4

THE BATTLE OF LONG TAN

August 1966

In August I participated in a monumental event, just two months after arriving in Vietnam. The month began in much the same way as July. I was on Kangaroo Courier every few days. Bruce and I got to fly the brigadier on a reconnaissance again on 1 August. We did not have to put him down anywhere this time, so he was not in danger of being left behind. I am not sure he knew that he had the same pilots he was so upset with a month before. He was looking around the area to the north of the Task Force.

I flew several routine trips each day over the next week. On 8 August I flew with the CO into Binh Ba where Operation Holdsworthy was in progress. Our task was to extract some VC prisoners. They were under Military Police guard, but we briefed our door gunners to keep a close eye on them and ensure none of them left a surprise packet behind as they got out. We had heard of cases in US helicopters where the departing prisoner had dropped a hand grenade, which obviously exploded some 15 to 20 seconds after they left the helicopter. We took two loads back to Nui Dat. It had been a successful resweep of this village-Operation Sydney had been carried out the previous month in the same area.

Bruce and I did another trip with prisoners a few days later. Then the next day Cliff and I brought out a wounded VC. The enemy seemed so innocuous. They were very small in stature, wore a flimsy black garment that was generally called 'pyjamas' as it consisted of a pullover shirt and trousers, and they were barefoot. Their smell was very strong and alien to us, generated by a rice diet and lack of hygiene. They cowered and were obviously terrified at being captured. Even when we were helping the wounded there was still a real fear in their eye. One wondered how we looked to them.

During Holdsworthy we seemed to get a lot more work and got to utilise our training skills in the variety of tasks we carried out to support the battalion.

On return from Nui Dat the next week we did some live firing of our door-mounted machine guns. We had grabbed a couple of wooden crates that we threw from the helicopter into the sea.

After the gunners had some practice I climbed into the back and had a go. It was amazing to look down the big arc of the bullets. We had included extra tracer rounds, whose fiery path you could see moving through the air and was used to help aiming. They created a line that left the aircraft and bent almost into a semi-circle. It was necessary to 'lead' the target by a large amount to have them hit the right area. This was due to the forward speed of the helicopter.

While we were shooting someone saw a large object in the water. Cliff decided to go down and investigate. It was a whale shark, probably about 15 metres in length. We hovered above its back and we could see it out the front and back of the helicopter.

'At least we'd have somewhere to land if the engine failed,' I quipped.

'I'm sure he'd take us back home,' Bluey responded in his dry style.

'Luckily, he wouldn't want to eat us,' Cliff said.

The next day was to become the most life changing in my Vietnam experience. In wartime, individuals can be thrust into experiences that call on them to use all their performance skills as well as display remarkable courage and valour. On this day we were required to carry out what looked to be a suicide mission in support of a surrounded and outnumbered company of 6RAR. That we survived is still one of those mysteries of battle.

The day started quite innocuously for me as I was told to carry out a compass swing on a helicopter that had been through some repairs. Bluey and I flew to a corner of the airfield where we were away from magnetic influences. He took readings from a datum compass as I rotated the helicopter through different aircraft compass headings. A chart of readings was then drawn up and placed on the instrument panel so any differences could be taken into account when navigating from one point to another.

Mid-morning, I joined with Frank plus Cliff and Bruce. We were the crews of two helicopters that were tasked to fly the first concert party from Australia up to the Task Force area.

'How about this! We get to meet Col Joye and Little Pattie!'

'Do you think they'll talk to us?' Bluey asked.

'Here's your big chance,' I said to Bluey. 'Here they come.'

'G'day, guys,' Col said. 'Thanks for giving us a ride.'

'All part of the service,' Frank said. 'How about an autograph?' he continued, obviously joking.

'Good one,' Col responded. 'Much danger where we're going?'

'No worries, it's been quiet for weeks,' we responded.

'Can I help you aboard?' Blue said to Little Pattie.

'Thanks,' is all she said. She appeared a little apprehensive.

'Put the gear in the other helicopter,' Frank said. 'We'll take a couple more passengers.'

The artists were a little apprehensive about the war zone and the degree of danger to them. We all told them there was nothing to worry about as there hadn't been any significant action in the first two months. They enjoyed the short flight and there were several willing diggers waiting to help them at the helipad. They disappeared and it was not very long before we started to hear the sounds of the guitarists tuning up.

As was our normal habit, we drifted up to the air operations tent. This was adjoining the Task Force headquarters. The air operations centre was generally manned by RAAF navigators, one of whom was Big Black, from my crew in the maritime squadron. It was always a good place to get a decent cup of coffee and catch up on what was going on around the province.

On this day people were a little nervous. The Task Force had been mortared in the early hours of the night before, giving our RAAF guys the first taste of being under fire. Luckily, none of them had been injured, although quite a few others had been and one engineer was to subsequently die from his wounds. There was also an air of uncertainty as people wondered what 'Charlie' was up to. They wondered whether he planned to come back again. Most of the stories were about who was where when the first round came. How they reacted. Who dived into which hole. How much water was in the hole.

'Delta Company has been sent out on a three-day patrol,' Black briefed us. 'Alpha Company is returning from their three-day patrol with no major sightings of the enemy to report. They did have a couple of contacts and brought in some local females for questioning. Charlie Company patrols to the south have nothing to report. Bravo Company found the launch sights for the mortar attack, just short of the Long Tan rubber.'

'What do you reckon is going on, Black?'

'The word is that it's just a small group causing us some flak,' he responded.

'No sign of a major attack?'

'Not that anyone can determine.'

'How did you go under attack?'

'I grabbed my weapons and dived into the hole,' he said. 'Only to find it had water in the bottom. The explosions were all 100 metres away. I had no idea of what was going to happen. It puts you a bit on edge.'

'A bit of a surprise for the Task Force?'

'Yes, no-one expected it.'

'How about a cup of coffee?' I asked changing the subject.

'No sweat. Over here. I'll put on the water.'

We chatted for a while and then walked back towards the helicopters down the muddy path through the rubber trees. The neat rows of trees in both directions with their canopy well above our heads provided the feeling of being under a big tent and walking down an avenue of tent poles. It was the monsoon season and it rained every afternoon towards evening.

Things were still very primitive in the Task Force area and raised pathways were a thing of the future. A primitive facility along this path was the toilet, a row of 'thunder boxes' as they were called, over an open trench and behind a hessian sheet. Grunting poles were provided and they doubled as a security hold against falling into the trench. Upon completion it was required that you threw a handful of lime into the hole to help keep down the smell.

Back at the helicopters we thought about lunch. Some decided to cook up a 'stew' from cans of hard rations. I walked back to the HQ dining tent and had some 'wholesome' army food, which had come out of bigger tins, with Big Black.

He was quite animated about the activity of the previous night and said he had got himself all set up to repel the invading hordes. After a cup of tea, he went back to work and I went back to the helicopters.

The music was starting at the concert and Frank and I walked in that direction to have a look. Everyone was cheering and quite excited by the whole affair. As was usual in the 1960s, the girls wore mini-mini-skirts and even though we had only been away for two months they were raising the temperature of most guys. Some were up dancing with each other in their greens and big boots. The tiny figure of Little Pattie with her blonde hair and blue mini was drawing lots of wolf whistles.

Suddenly the 105-millimetre artillery to our west fired a mission. This surprised everyone as it was not anticipated that they would fire during the concert. But the concert went on as it was drawing to its conclusion anyway.

Then they fired several times. It was obvious something unusual was happening. I followed

Frank to the operations tent as he went to see if he could find out what it was. We soon discovered that Delta Company had made contact with a small number of enemy. They were in pursuit. We hung around listening to the radios. It was about a quarter to four.

The contact quickly escalated as 11 Platoon was fired upon by a greater number of enemy. Then 10 Platoon was engaged as it tried to move to their assistance. The artillery had become a regimental mission, with all guns firing. The noise was deafening and continued incessantly for the next few hours. The concert had finished and some soldiers were taking the concert party to look around. Little Pattie was sitting up on an armoured personnel carrier as she drove around. Suddenly there was a call to arms and everyone raced off to their respective action stations. I discovered later that another helicopter arrived and flew her back to Vung Tau. Col Joye was not so lucky as he missed the ride and spent the night with the diggers as they waited for the enemy to attack.

We stayed in the operations area within earshot of the radios, but remained clear of the headquarters staff and the brigadier. Frank was keen to get into the action. He was waiting for an opportunity.

The Task Force was actually quite undermanned at that instant as 5RAR were to the north and not due to return till the next day. The companies of 6RAR had been patrolling. Alpha Company had just arrived back in camp after three days out. Bravo Company had been sent out for a morning patrol. They were then ordered to stay overnight without rations or equipment. Half their number had been sent back to camp to go on overdue R&R at Vung Tau. Charlie Company was on perimeter defensive duty around the Task Force area.

When a relief force was considered the only possibility was Alpha Company. They were told to get ready to go out again. The APC Squadron was told to get carriers ready to lift Alpha Company into the Long Tan rubber plantation. But no order to move was given to this relief force for the next hour and a half as the brigadier appeared to want to see what the intentions of the enemy would be. Maybe they were going to attack the Task Force area and he did not want to be without any defensive troops.

I found it fascinating watching the action, tension and stress that were generated in this headquarters. The urgency with which Harry (OC Delta Company) was requesting support left no doubt in anyone's mind that he was in serious trouble.

I remember hearing at one stage when there was some delay in responding to his request.

'If you don't fuckin' give me what I want, you might as well forget my men. And get ready to be killed yourselves. Now fuckin' hurry up.'

While he requested reinforcements and was told they were on the way, he was not to know that they had not left the Task Force area.

He asked for air support and was told that US fighter bombers were overhead. Unfortunately, neither the FAC (forward air controller) aircraft nor the fighters could see the battle area through the cloud. Harry decided that the artillery was more important. The brief break in their firing was cancelled. The situation became progressively worse. Harry reported the loss of the 11 Platoon commander. Then more and more men. He began to attempt to withdraw everyone into a defensive position. The survivors of 11 Platoon were cut off. Harry sent part of 12 Platoon to rescue them.

After about an hour, Harry started to call for an ammunition resupply. They had only taken the normal 60 rounds per man and this was disappearing. The brigadier raised the question of how this could be achieved. He looked to the RAAF air commander. He asked if he could provide helicopters. The group captain responded that it was outside the operational directives for the use of 9 Squadron. He did not think it would be possible. The brigadier was furious and turned to the US air commander. He said they could do it. But it would take at least half an hour to get helicopters to the area.

This was Frank's cue. My brave, courageous and foolhardy skipper stepped forward and said he would do it.

'I'll go,' Frank said. 'I am tactical commander of the helicopter. I decide what it can and cannot do. I say we go.'

'Can he really do that?' the brigadier asked, looking at the group captain.

'Are you sure, Frank?' he said. 'This is flying into an unsafe area.'

'I would prefer to try than do nothing,' he responded.

'Maybe we should check with higher authority.'

'They will only fuck around and waste time,' Frank said. 'It's my helicopter in this situation and I say we go.'

'I guess you're right,' he said.

'About time someone in the RAAF showed some guts,' the brigadier responded. 'Get over to Eagle Farm and load up. Radio Harry and tell him ammunition is on the way.'

I did not instantly agree.

'How the hell are we going to do this?' I asked Frank.

'We just will, forget it,' he said.

'But there are hordes out there, Frank. It's impossible.'

'You don't have to come,' he responded. 'Volunteers only.'

'I'm with you,' Bruce responded.

'Me too,' Cliff said, but perhaps with a little less conviction.

'Of course I'll come,' I said. 'But how are we going to pull it off?'

We were walking quickly back along the path to the helicopters. The guns were firing continuously. I was yelling to make myself heard.

'This is madness, Frank,' I continued. 'What's your plan?'

'We'll use the SAS tactics,' he said. 'We'll fly out at height, find them and then guide Cliff in.'

'But we have no defences, Frank. What chance have we got against their weapons?'

'Stop shitting me, Bob. Let's not worry about it.'

'But I am. I don't want to die doing something stupid. We need to plan a way to get the ammunition in without too much danger to us. One hit and our helicopter will just blow up.'

'Fuckin' shut up,' was his response.

This did not help me one bit. As we continued to move back down the muddy path I still wanted to discuss the issue.

'This is madness, Frank,' I said. 'It's suicidal. It will achieve nothing.'

He didn't care what I was saying; he was off to win a medal. Despite all my protestations there was never any delay by anyone in carrying out their duties and moving out. The other pilots and crew just accepted the inevitability of their role and went about their professional actions. I was a questioner by nature and did not blindly accept any direction. I was one who wanted to think everything through. I wanted to try to see all the angles. I continued to mutter about the insanity of what we were doing for some time.

When we arrived at Eagle Farm the RSM, George, had just arrived and started to mobilise everybody into a human chain moving boxes of ammunition from the store. As the boxes arrived discussion developed about what to do with them. Whether to cut the steel bands. Whether to open the boxes and load magazines. Whether blankets should be included for the wounded. It was decided to break the bands and wrap the boxes in a blanket. This way the maximum amount could be loaded. Also, it would all be ready in the quickest time.

Although we had shut down the engines we kept the radios on and listened to the action. Harry was becoming more and more agitated. He was obviously more and more desperate. It was now 5.30 and the relief force finally moved out of the Task Force area on its way. This was a delay of more than an hour. A similar time that it was to take them to get to Delta Company. Similarly, we were loaded and waiting but did not get the nod to take off till just before six. I remember being very nervous during this time and concerned for my survival.

The two crews decided to use the same tactics that we had developed for working with the SAS. As the lead helicopter we would fly out at height and locate the drop point. Then we would guide the other helicopter in at treetop level. Once they had dropped their load of boxes we would dive down and drop our load. At least these tactics maximised my chances of survival, I thought.

The back of the helicopters were stacked full of boxes and then someone asked how they would fall out. The RSM decide he would jump on board and do the job. The company 2IC (second-in-charge) then decided he would come too. Two volunteers jumped into the other helicopter. We all then waited some more.

Finally, the artillery stopped and we were cleared to go. We lifted off and headed east. What greeted our eyes as we reached the top of the trees was devastating. There was a blinding monsoon rain storm in our path. We could not climb to height. Almost immediately we were in the rain. We could not see anything, so slowed down to about 20 knots. We very slowly moved east. I was navigating by looking down between my feet through the perspex. I saw a road that turned through 90 degrees from east to south.

'There's the bend in the road at Long Tan,' I said. 'We're behind enemy lines. Turn back east, quickly.' I had been scared; now I was terrified.

Someone said, 'Did you hear that?' as a bullet whistled past.

'Nina-four throw smoke,' I radioed.

'Roger. Smoke thrown,' was the response. They were obviously waiting for us. They were missing the artillery that provided a shield of exploding steel around their position.

'I see orange smoke.'

'Wrong, wrong,' was the response.

Frank quickly banked the helicopter and turned to the south. My heart gave a flutter and

I drew myself into a smaller ball within the armour-plated seat.

'The bastards must be awake to us. They are trying to fool us into dropping the ammunition to them.'

'Nina-four throw smoke,' I radioed again.

'Smoke thrown.'

'I see red smoke.'

'Roger, roger,' came the anxious reply. It was from the same position.

We then turned to the west to locate the other helicopter. All this time we were only a little above the treetops, in blinding rain and travelling at slow speed.

'I'm having trouble seeing you, Cliff,' Frank said. 'Turn on your anti-collision light.' We saw the red light on top of the helicopter through the rain.

'Turn left. Roll out now,' Frank instructed Cliff. 'Right 10 degrees, 300 metres to run. That's it. Flare now. You're on top. Drop your load.'

The helicopter rolled on its side and the boxes went tumbling down towards the ground. They headed west towards home. We then flew over the spot and rolled onto our side. The guys in the back gave the boxes a kick with their feet and they went tumbling out the open door.

'Here comes another load,' I called.

'Right on! You beauty,' came the call over the radio.

To which my intrepid skipper quickly replied, 'All part of the service,' as we also headed west.

There euphoric chatter in the helicopter as we realised that we had completed the mission and were heading back alive. I could not believe that we had not taken any hits.

The artillery started again as we landed at 6RAR to drop off our passengers. We flew on to Kangaroo Pad and headed up to the operations tent. It was later that we learned that many soldiers in the battle had actually run out of ammunition or were about to when our drop arrived. It was one of the major turning points in their ability to survive further waves of enemy assaults. I had not seen anything of the troops on the ground. Others felt they saw our guys wallowing around in the mud. But nobody saw any sign of the enemy. There had been a couple of whistling noises that sounded like bullets passing close to the helicopter. It all added to the puzzle of the situation. Hopefully we would find out more at operations.

When we arrived we found the CO had arrived. He was pleased to see that we had returned safely. He was a little upset with our decision to go without his knowledge. We were congratulated for the safe and accurate delivery of the ammunition. We were then told to return to our helicopters and wait for further orders. It was disappointing to move away from the sound of the radio traffic as we now had a personal attachment to the beleaguered company. We could hear that the radio chatter was much quieter now. All the guns were still firing incessantly. We reluctantly strolled back to our helicopter. When we arrived we saw that the rest of the squadron had arrived to join us.

It was starting to get dark. We were told that we were on standby to return and do a medivac of the wounded soldiers. Those who were interested went off to have a meal. That included me, as I was always ready to eat. We chatted to the other squadron members. There was not a lot to tell. Mainly, that we got back when we were not expecting to return. The noise of the artillery was still horrendous, with seemingly continuous loud explosions as all guns fired one after the other. We told the story as we had pieced it together from listening to the radios. The artillery was creating a wall of metal through which the VC was attacking. It was having a devastating effect. Our troops had run out of ammunition and that had been our role to provide a resupply. That Alpha Company in APCs was on their way out to provide reinforcements.

After dinner we returned to the pad and sat around our helicopters. There had been talk that maybe the VC had a second regiment that was positioning to the north and would provide a pincer-movement-type attack. This would have been the force that the last two operations in the area around Binh Ba had tried to find. A report came in that one of the US Chinooks had taken fire from the west. These Chinooks were providing a continuous resupply of artillery ammunition for the guns from Vung Tau. This made us all feel a bit nervous as we thought of the consequences of a mortar attack on the landing pad where our whole squadron was parked.

'All this crap about secure locations,' Frank said. 'We're obviously within their mortar range. They could wipe us all out with a couple of bombs. We should be up doing something. Or fucking off to Vung Tau and coming back when we're needed.'

'Just be patient, Frank,' Laddie said. 'You'll get your chance to see action again before long. You're lucky to still be here to have another go.'

'Bullshit. Nobody's going to put a hole in my bum,' was Frank's reply.

As the hours drifted past we wondered what was happening. The rate of fire of the artillery started to ease. It was obvious that the big American guns were now firing out to a more distant target. While it was not so incessant, the gunfire continued till close to midnight. This was a total of nearly seven hours before it was stopped for us to go in for the wounded.

The CO came down during the evening and explained that we were waiting for those in the battle area to withdraw to a location for us to land. We just had to sit and wait. The chatter continued. A whole range of enemy attack scenarios were aired. Then elaborate plans for our escape were detailed. We brewed tea and coffee on the hexamine stoves that were in our ration packs.

Close to midnight an American Dust-off helicopter arrived and joined us. The CO called everyone to a briefing.

'The troops have withdrawn to a cleared area on the western side of the rubber,' he said. 'We don't know if the enemy are still in the area or planning a counter attack. So that we don't give away their position, we won't use landing lights as we come into their position.'

'Do you want us to go in first?' asked the US Dust-off skipper.

'Yes. You have the specialist gear on board,' he replied. 'Take the most seriously injured.'

'Roger.'

'I'll go next,' he continued. 'Then I want each of you to take off as the preceding helicopter clears the area. Laddie, you can organise an order. Take your time and good luck.'

The word came and the Dust-off helicopter started up. Laddie came over to us and said that he was sending us in last.

'I think you've done your bit, Frank,' he said. 'We'll only use you if necessary.'

'Shit, mate. I want to go back in,' Frank replied.

'Let's see,' Laddie said, using his typical response.

This did not please Frank, who was determined to be part of the action. It was a very black night as the rain clouds were still around. It was not going to be an easy task to locate and approach a jungle pad. This was despite the fact that it was only a bit more than 2 kilometres away.

We all sat in our helicopters waiting our turn. Once again, we spoke about the element of danger and the unknown. It was going to be necessary to work well as a team if we were going to carry out this task safely and efficiently. We decided that the crewmen would maintain watch to the sides for obstacles. I would look down the approach path and call rates of descent and watch beneath the helicopter through the windscreen under my feet. Frank would maintain a close watch on the instruments in a similar fashion to a ground-controlled approach. We had the radios on to listen to the activity of the other helicopters. It seemed a very long time as we sat waiting for our turn.

Suddenly there was a huge light in the sky that quickly disappeared. The US helicopter had used their landing light, despite the order not to. They quickly departed with those who needed the most urgent attention. Then the CO did his approach and headed off to the hospital at Vung Tau. One by one the rest of the squadron carried out their approach. It was obviously quite difficult as the chatter on the radio indicated that some were having trouble locating the landing zone. Others were having trouble on the approach, trying several times before landing safely. Finally, it was our turn to take off.

Once again it was as black as pitch as we headed east. We could see the anti-collision light of the helicopter ahead, which helped us locate the general area. It suddenly disappeared into the jungle. We continued forward, and it soon reappeared as it lifted off again.

'Can anyone see the lights of the landing pad?' Frank asked.

'Can't see a thing,' I said.

'There's something over there, Skip. To the left,' Bluey said.

'I'm starting a descent,' Frank said. 'Keep your eyes open.'

'We're going down pretty fast, Frank,' I said. 'I suggest we slow down a bit. What's the rate of descent?'

'It's OK,' Frank responded.

'There's a small tree to the right, boss,' Bluey called.

'Looks clear underneath, Frank. Bring her down.'

Frank slowly but surely descended into the abyss. We landed just in front of the APC. A soldier moved forward to Frank's window.

'All the wounded have gone,' he said. 'There are some bodies if you want to take them.'

'OK,' Frank replied.

The bodies were wrapped in groundsheets. They had already started to take on that distinctive smell of rotting flesh. Half a dozen were piled into the back and we prepared to take off. The first sight of dead bodies made the reality of war jump out at me. It was so easy to go from living to dead. You would never know when it was going to happen. It was close to 12.30am as we lifted the last load up into the air. We climbed vertically up to the top of the trees.

Just as we were about to move forward the whole sky and area in front of us lit up from massive explosions. There were fireballs, shockwaves and loud thunderous noises.

'Hold the artillery,' I radioed on the battalion net. 'We're still in the area.'

'Are you OK, Frank?' It was the CO's voice.

'Roger, some bastards have started to open fire again. Before we're away.'

'No artillery fire,' came over the battalion net.

It was later reported that it was a medium level bomber that had offloaded its ordinance on the hill just to our north, about 2000 metres away. It gave us an incredible fright.

As we flew back to the hospital the artillery recommenced. It was firing at targets along suspected withdrawal routes for the enemy. Ten minutes later we landed at the morgue and the bodies were taken inside. We then flew back to our squadron pad and closed down. Jeeps were waiting and took us to the dining hall where our cooks had stayed up and prepared a steak and beer meal as we arrived home. The adrenaline of the day meant that we were still very alert at one in the morning, although I certainly slept soundly once I hit the cot.

This was our first real taste of war. We had been in Vietnam for two months and had not been involved in enemy action to this point. Would the rest of our tour be more like this? This was dangerous stuff. Did we do enough? Could we have done more? Would we have to go back in the morning and do some more? How were those that survived and were still in the jungle? We pondered these unanswerable questions as we walked back to Villa Anna to retire in the early hours of the morning.

The Battle of Long Tan was the most significant battle fought by Australians in Vietnam and one that is regarded as the highest performance battle of the war by John Pimlott in his book *Vietnam: The Decisive Battles*. His measurement is based on the number of troops on each side, the number of casualties and the duration of the battle.

There were 108 in Delta Company 6RAR, and an estimated 2500-plus enemy soldiers. A total of 18 friendly soldiers lost their lives. While the official enemy body count was stopped at 250, it is known that there were many more killed or died subsequently from graves found on follow-up operations and VC hospital records. The duration of the battle was approximately three hours, meaning a quick and decisive defeat was inflicted upon the enemy. This defeat was so decisive that the Australian Task Force Base was not again attacked, nor was it challenged by such a large enemy force.

The papers back in Australia published articles headlined 'RAAF Heroism-Copters turned tide of battle'.

RAAF HEROISM
'Copters turned tide of battle

CANBERRA, Mon. — RAAF helicopter crews may never hear a happier sound than a radio voice which crackled through the rain-swept blackness over the Baria battlefield last Thursday night.

"YOU bloody beaut... that was smack on," the voice said.

This was the signal that ammunition two 'copter crews dropped to hard-pressed Diggers was right on target.

And, as the review of battle showed, the drop not only saved the troops from annihilation but helped them to valiant victory.

The battle already is history.

A powerful Communist force had surrounded D Company, Sixth Battalion, Australian Task Force, in Vietnam.

The Communists sprang the trap when D Company, on routine patrol, was passing through a rubber plantation near Baria, about 40 miles south-east of Saigon.

Attacked

The Australians, attacked from all sides, quickly exhausted their ammunition in fighting off wave after wave of the charging enemy.

They radioed Task Force headquarters to send more ammunition.

This call brought the RAAF into the action.

RAAF headquarters, in Canberra, tonight released details of the part No. 9 Squadron played in supporting the embattled patrol.

Two Iroquois helicopters of the squadron, piloted by Flight - Lieutenant Cliff Dohle, of Canberra, and Frank Riley, of Victoria, flew ammunition supplies to the battle area.

In torrential monsoonal rain they flew low over the battlefield, searching for a wisp of smoke—the arranged signal—that would guide them to the company's position.

Flight - Lieutenant Bob Grandin, of Queenscliffe (Victoria), saw smoke coming from a rubber plantation.

But the helicopters could not find a landing place and their crews had to drop the ammunition through the rubber trees to the soldiers below.

They were right on target.

Over the radio came a voice from the ground "You bloody beaut, that was smack on."

Evacuation

Other helicopters of No. 9 Squadron waited at task force headquarters, ready for instant action.

A second call for help came from D Company just before midnight — to evacuate wounded.

By the dim lights of the relieving A Company's Armoured personnel carrying the squadron CO Wing-Commander Ray Scott, of Wagga (N.S.W.) landed his helicopter on a rough pad hastily prepared in the battle area.

After Wing-Commander Scott had taken out the first wounded, other helicopters of the squadron...

The final body count of 245 enemy dead was reached yesterday afternoon with the discovery of 14 bodies in a shallow jungle grave.

The patrols also found a camp the retreating Communist force used as a casualty clearing station.

A large stock of medical supplies and equipment was lying about the camp.

SAIGON, Mon. — Elements of the Fifth and Sixth Battalions, RAR, last night ended "Operation Smithfield," in which they killed 245 Communists.

The search and destroy operation followed last Thursday's Baria battle — the biggest Australian troops have fought since the Korean war.

For the last three days Australian patrols have scoured the jungle for remnants of the Communist force the Sixth Battalion's D company routed in the battle.

The final body count of 245 enemy dead was reached yesterday afternoon with the discovery of 14 bodies in a shallow jungle grave.

The patrols also found a camp the retreating Communist force used as a casualty clearing station.

A large stock of medical supplies and equipment was lying about the camp.

Unknown paper and date
circa 22 Aug '66

'RAAF Heroism—'Copters turned tide of battle', Unknown paper, circa 22 August 1966.

***

The next day, 19 August, I was flying again. Ted and I did a mission dropping leaflets along the probable withdrawal paths of the VC who had been involved in the previous day's battle. The leaflets offered money to any VC who was willing to surrender. They got extra money if they brought a weapon with them. As we opened the boxes of leaflets and placed them near the door the circulation of the air drew them out of the boxes and scattered them everywhere.

Another aspect of the activity over the preceding days confronted my wife at home. One of the mailmen from Nui Dat lived over the back fence of my house in Canberra. When he was injured in the mortar attack on the base, it gave my wife quite a fright to see the padre visiting his wife to tell her the news. History had created the image that this visit was normally associated with death. It was a visit all wives dreaded. Obviously, this was a tension for our families throughout the time we were away.

FAMILY AID

The family car won't start, the hot water system is playing up, and one of the kids looks like going down with the 'flu.

A familiar enough situation in many families, you would say. But imagine the extra worry when Dad is away in Vietnam.

Members of the RAAF Base Fairbairn, Canberra, realizing the problems for the wife, and for the absent husband, have set up a family assistance scheme to care for those families.

Each family with a RAAF husband away in Vietnam has been allotted a contact from among the members remaining at Fairbairn. The responsibility of the contact man, each one a volunteer, is to liaise regularly with the family, and without necessarily waiting to be asked, arrange to have those small jobs fixed around the house normally looked after by the husband, perhaps the babies minded while Mum goes to the doctors, or shopping, and other small, but necessary, chores.

The system is based on the principle that many wives are known to be loathe to ask for assistance, except in the case of dire emergency, yet quite often a simple matter such as the repair of a dripping tap or a broken toy, can make all the difference to her peace of mind.

The family contact will call regularly at the home allotted to him, and will note any jobs needing attention. These will then be looked after by a group of volunteers on the base, who between them will tackle tasks from motor car repairs and wood chopping, to baby minding and minor house repairs.

● Sgt Doug Perkins, transport fitter, shows Mrs Norma Lucas why her car wouldn't start. Her husband, Sgt Bill Lucas, an armament fitter, is with the RAAF in Vietnam.

Members of the WRAAF at Fairbairn are on the volunteer list, and will take over the chores most suited to female temperaments. If necessary, they will cook and wash if the wife is sick.

RAAF men of No 9 Squadron left Australia for Vietnam a month ago, and already the scheme is well under way. In that time the organization has provided assistance for:—

● repair of a house occupied by a RAAF family;
● advice and assistance on car repairs;
● hospital visits, and convalescent care for sick wife;
● enquiries on allotments and other administration details.

The RAAF is assisting the families officially by allowing them to remain in the married quarters or Government house for the period the husband is away. Some of the families are living in houses on the base, and more are occupying homes in Canberra suburbs.

The family contacts are chosen with care, almost always are already a friend of the family, and mostly live in close proximity to them.

The three Messes on the base are doing their part in the scheme by inviting the wives to all social functions in the respective Messes.

These voluntary arrangements are not only proving invaluable to the wives and families left behind, but are going a long way to easing the minds of the RAAF men with No 9 Squadron in Vietnam.

● Mrs Margaret Banfield, wife of Flt Lt Geoff Banfield, a helicopter pilot in Vietnam, leaves her two young children with off-duty WRAAF Charlene Glover, while she goes shopping. The Banfields live at Ainslie, Canberra.

'Family Aid', RAAF News, August 1966.

In an effort to support the wives and provide a 'husband' replacement each family was allocated a 'buddy' from amongst those still working back in Canberra. They were only a telephone call away and also visited each week to assist with any small tasks, as well as provide general moral support during this difficult time.

The rest of August involved routine missions. I did another leaflet drop. Several Kangaroo Couriers. A SAS insertion and extraction. Troop movements and a medivac. I did a total of 43 hours and 50 minutes with 251 sorties. That means one take-off and landing every 10 minutes of flying time, on average.

Three days after Long Tan I celebrated my 26th birthday. Laddie gave me the day off task.

'Come on, Bob, I'll take you downtown for lunch,' Frank said.

We strolled down to the centre of town where there were several food carts lined along the street.

'How can you be sure of what you're eating and what it will do to you?' I asked Frank.

'We do this all the time in Butterworth,' he replied. 'They use so many spices and curries that it kills any bugs. Have a go.'

Frank ordered an array of foods that we ate at a sidewalk table. We also bought some local beer to help wash it all down. It proved to be tasty, but certainly there was no way to determine exactly what it was. I survived and thanked Frank for an interesting experience.

TRAVELLING A FULL CIRCLE

It was quite a shock when I was posted back to the Air Force Academy after two years in Butterworth. The role of flight commander was an administrative one, but it was also one of leadership and example. I had had a wide range of experiences and could share these with the cadets. I enjoyed intellectual challenge and academic work. I still pursued an active sporting career. I had strong ideas on the leadership of men, some of which were not aligned with established service tradition. Would this regimental establishment cope with my return? I was excited by the prospect of going back as I liked all that it stood for.

I decided that I would immerse myself in the life of a cadet and went back to class to complete my science degree. I also became fully involved in sport, to the extent that I both coached and played in the cadet rugby team. I found that I was really enjoying the role of mentoring the cadets. My familiarity and popularity with the cadets created some tension with other officers who struggled to recognise the balance of respect that I was able to maintain. I also championed the cadet's position on many irritating points of procedure. As the only veteran of Vietnam I also found that I had a less than tolerant attitude towards the other officers and their desire to ensure rigid conformity and formal routines. I believed we needed cadets who could think for themselves and show initiative.

I performed quite outstandingly in my academic endeavours while maintaining my full-time administrative position. I also captain-coached the Air Force Australian Rules football and rugby teams, achieving combined service representation. It was just like being back at college again. The personal power that I felt set me on a path to challenge my role in the air force. While I personally felt that I had a lot to offer in a changing and developing service, I was seen by some as a difficult person to deal with and a 'loose cannon'.

The principal problem I felt was that I would not have any control over the direction my life would take. For example, we were briefed on the move by the air force to introduce a computer management system. I put myself forward to work in this department as the only person currently in the air force to have studied Information Science. The briefing officers had been keen for my involvement. It was rejected to my astonishment. (I later learned that they sent an officer from the course after me to the

USA to do basically the same computer course that I had completed.) I then asked to return to helicopters and be part of the pick-up of the new Chinook helicopter. I was told I could not bargain for a posting but must do as I was directed. I became frustrated and angry.

Progressively I recognised that I would not achieve satisfaction within the service. I needed to resign my commission. After 16 years, with only four to go before I gained a pension, it was a major rift and one my family and friends found difficult to understand. The anger and frustration within me did not allow me to tolerate the impersonal approach to management. Life had become something that could be taken in an instant and one that should not be wasted doing things you did not want to do.

At that time the pension was an insignificant amount of money and one on which I could not support a family. (Little did I know that a new government would change the whole profile of retirement benefits in the following year.) I was confident that I would find employment that I enjoyed and which would maximise my time with my family. After investigating computer analysis with IBM, flying airlines and helicopters, I chose the lower paying job of teaching. I loved the interaction with young people and the college life. I was appointed to the staff of one of the Greater Public Schools in Melbourne, Carey Baptist Grammar School.

Thus began my second career teaching in schools, which was to span the next 25 years. When asked by the principal what I hoped to do in teaching, I responded that I wanted to teach children who hated school. I worked through from my position as a mathematics teacher to head of mathematics and then principal during my time in teaching, always championing the challenge of teaching the underachieving child. The two schools of which I was principal were predominantly for children unsettled in the traditional education system, although I was gradually able to show that other ways of presenting the curriculum also improved the performance of the 'normal' child.

We bought a suburban block of land, took out a war service loan and built our 'dream' home. It was two-storey, looked across the river parkland to the city and I put in a swimming pool. But it was not to be a story of a settled and peaceful life. I felt closed in by the surrounding houses. I did not enjoy the interaction with close neighbours. When two young children were abducted from the suburb I felt an uncontrollable insecurity within this environment. We did not feel we could allow our children to play unsupervised in a small park just two doors down the street.

After six months in our new house we went to the hills, the Dandenong Ranges, and bought a 10-acre (4-hectare) block of tea-tree scrub. We sold our house, lost our war service loan, and moved into a caravan. Over the next three years we built a log cabin-style house and a great little farm that provided many of our needs. Despite having to drive for an hour to and from work each day it was a blissful existence. The children were able to walk a few hundred metres up the country road to a little one-room school.

By the end of the fourth year I was struggling with the routine of the existence, wanted to have a bigger farm and ambitiously looked to having more control in the delivery of the curriculum. Despite the tranquillity and security of our situation I gave notice that I would leave at the end of the following year and searched for a country school to move on to. Once again, I astounded my parents and friends by causing disruption to the stable existence and settled appearance we had.

I gained a position at The Armidale School in New South Wales and we moved our menagerie of animals in a two-vehicle convoy during a blistering heatwave across the breadth of two states. We had purchased 120 acres (over 50 hectares) about 15 minutes outside the town and had a house built for us this time. The majority of things were going well for our family. The children were attending good private schools and enjoyed the space of the property. Jan was successfully raising fat lambs and enjoyed her trips to the market.

I had enrolled in a Master's degree course, joined the Army Reserve to command the university infantry company, was teaching an aviation course at the TAFE and enjoyed my appointment to the role of head of mathematics at the school. But one day, while I was a guest teaching a group of mathematicians at university, a senior maths teacher spoke to me about how much he envied my life and wanted to get out of Sydney. I, on the other hand, felt very tired of it all. I offered him my job and when he said he was serious I went back to school and resigned my job, telling the head that I had a replacement organised. He was astounded but supported my need for a break.

I had been in Armidale for two and a half years. I took a position flying a charter aircraft part time, and purchased a 2500-acre (1000-hectare) property in a remote location between Armidale and Inverell. I felt a great sense of tranquillity in the isolation.

We moved back into a caravan. I purchased a few angora stud bucks and a couple of semitrailer loads of female wild goats and let them go together. With visions of them back-breeding to a herd of angora goats I went off on air charter trips and slept all day under the wing of the aircraft as I waited for my passengers. After six months it was obvious that we were fast approaching financial ruin. We entered a drought cycle, which reduced funds available for chartering aircraft. Returns from the goats did not reach the forecast levels. It was a glorious adventure, but I recognised that it was based upon little rational thought.

I was lucky enough to get a position as deputy principal of the Longreach Pastoral College. But expecting to maintain the property for the next two years from a position 1600 kilometres away was unrealistic. Living in the isolation of the outback with a failing goat farm was not a reasonable existence for my family so I again resigned and took a teaching job in Brisbane. We sold the farm, and bought a suburban house and a small gift shop for Jan.

I continued to look for an opportunity where I could exercise the flexibility that I felt was important for students. I wanted to run a school and focus on the needs of the students as a diverse body of learners. I wanted to work in a school that helped the students who did not 'fit the system' and were having an unsatisfactory experience. But I was generally frustrated by the rigidity of a traditional approach. My drive and desire, with the help of my current principal, landed me a job at a small farm school that was struggling to survive in Far North Queensland.

'Next move may be away', The Sun, 17 November 1966.

CHAPTER 5

SEARCHING FOR THE ENEMY

September to December 1966

The experience in Vietnam was never the same after the Battle of Long Tan. We had been blooded and reminded how this was about 'kill or be killed'. Following Frank's voluntary involvement in a hostile activity it was hard for the squadron not to become involved in more dangerous missions. The squadron had been tested and came through with a perfect performance. Despite lingering discontent associated with command and control within the upper echelons, the diggers at the 'sharp end' developed a great affinity for our helicopters and the tasks we could perform for them.

September began the process of searching for the enemy to complete his routing within Phuoc Tuy Province. He proved to be very elusive and only small groups came into contact with the Australians over the next ten months. Operations roved further from Nui Dat. Our support role in these circumstances became busier. The SAS took their reconnaissance patrols closer to the provincial borders. Winning the hearts and minds of the locals also became a part of our role.

We took responsibility for the Dust-off Standby helicopter at Task Force. Medical evacuation (medivac) was one of the most important roles that we played in Vietnam. The call sign for these operations was 'Dust-off. Involvement in medical evacuation situations arose both impromptu, where a passing helicopter was diverted to provide assistance, and as tasking for the helicopter on standby at the medical aid post LZ.

Initially the US helicopters with their big red cross on the side were tasked to stand by our major operations as they were well equipped for the task with specialist crewmen and winches to lift the injured through the jungle. After a short while winches became available and we were able to fit the appropriate equipment to carry out the task ourselves. I always believed that one of the great assets of the helicopter to the soldier in battle was that he had a high chance of being in a hospital inside a very short space of time and getting high quality treatment of his wounds.

***

There's no doubt that we lived a much more comfortable life at Vung Tau than the diggers at Nui Dat, returning to our villa each night from the 'war'. But it did not reduce the risk that we faced each time we left Vung Tau and flew on tasks within the province. Despite the many hours of waiting between flights, each mission was one in which we faced the ever-present danger of being shot. This tension affected everyone differently, but it created a daily lifestyle in which people were tense, exhausted, intoxicated and asleep. With just six crews and one on stand-down, we usually flew on some form of task each day.

Two crews were at Nui Dat on Kangaroo Standby each day. September began for me with two of these days flying with Dave. After breakfast, just before dawn, we drove the jeep out to the airfield.

'There's a major push by US forces in Long Khanh Province to the north of Phuoc Tuy, mainly around Xuan Loc,' the operations officer briefed us. 'The Task Force has the role of providing a blocking force at the provincial boundary near the Courtney rubber plantation. You can expect several trips into this location on battalion support.'

'Has there been any contact with the enemy?' Dave asked.

'Not by our troops; however, the Yanks have had a few torrid encounters. As usual, you need to keep a good lookout as you fly up Route 2 as there have been several hit-and-run ambushes along this road. The last one was the day before yesterday, late in the afternoon.'

'Bob, you go out and pre-flight the helicopter; I'll be there in a minute,' Dave directed.

Bluey and Brian, the crewmen, were already at the helicopter. They had collected the ammunition and placed the M60 machine guns on the mounts at the side.

'G'day, guys. Recovered from that party last night?' I taunted.

'No sweat; actually got to bed early. It was before midnight,' Bluey responded.

'I got on to some extra rations, knowing what a "munger" merchant you are,' said Brian.

'Sounds good. Did you get any of those chocolate bars that you had last time?'

'No, but I got some biscuits that they say are digestible.'

Dave arrived as I finished the check.

'Let's get going; we have an early request to take the 2IC up to the battalion at Courtney first thing.'

We put on our armour-plated vests and then the flak jacket over the top of it. Despite it being a pretty hot get-up, we wouldn't travel without it. Together with the armour-plated seat the gear gave us some protection in what is really a very vulnerable cockpit with only perspex in front and under us.

'Albatross 21 for departure north,' I radioed as Dave lifted off and we headed up the peninsula on the 25-kilometre journey that took ten minutes to Nui Dat.

The 2IC was waiting at Kangaroo and we continued on our journey north up Route 2. It was a graded dirt track with some pedestrian traffic and the occasional bullock cart. Adjacent to the road there were rubber plantations cleared from the jungle. After a few kilometres we flew over the ARVN fortress at Binh Bah South and then the township of Binh Gia. The Australians spent many operations attempting to secure these locations from Viet Cong infiltration.

The next 10 kilometres to Courtney plantation were over similar terrain, but it was less secure and under Viet Cong influence. We flew at 2000 feet, a height at which we were less likely to be hit by small arms fire from the ground. The Courtney plantation had a long history under French influence and was reported to have a peaceful understanding with the Viet Cong. What that meant we were never quite sure. Our troops were stationed to the east of the plantation and we dropped the 2IC off at the headquarters area before taking a couple of injured diggers back to Nui Dat with us.

We had time for a brew before we were tasked to do a courier run to ALSG at the back beach of Vung Tau taking a couple of diggers on R&C and returning with a load of supplies. We then returned to Courtney to collect the 2IC. This took us to lunch time. After lunch we took a couple of loads of supplies to the battalion at Courtney as arranged by the 2IC before hanging around for the rest of the afternoon. Just before dusk we flew back to Vung Tau. It was a 10-hour day in which we were airborne for one hour and 50 minutes and did 11 take-offs and landings.

On 2 September, while I was on Kangaroo Standby, a parade was carried out by Delta Company 6RAR for a visiting South Vietnamese general who wanted to present medals from his government in recognition of the valour shown by the company on the day of the Battle of Long Tan. After he arrived, the Australian Ambassador, who had come down for the parade, told him that approval had not been received from the Queen and the presentation could not go ahead.

This was most embarrassing and created quite a diplomatic incident. It has become a part of an ongoing saga involving awards to those who fought the Battle. While the proposed awards were listed in Australian newspapers, the Australian Government did not recognise their existence until July 2004 (38 years later), after the publication of the book *The Battle of Long Tan as told by the Commanders to Bob Grandin* (A&U) and just prior to an election.

The troops had to stay at the parade area and wait for the matter to be sorted out. The general sent aides to the nearest village and they bought dolls in traditional Vietnamese dresses and cigar cases. The parade was assembled and these were presented. Frank and I got a doll each.

***

On Sunday, Frank and I flew a medical team into Binh Gia, the village to the north of the Task Force area. The local priest had organised that mothers would bring their children for medical check-ups. As we arrived they were all waiting in the town centre.

'Looks like a good turnout,' Frank commented.

'I hope none run out as we come in to land.'

'Get out quick and take control of the rotor, Blue,' continued Frank. 'And keep them back from the chopper.'

'Right, Skip.'

'Tell them we'll show them the helicopter after their medical check,' Frank said to the medical team. 'Otherwise you may not get to see them. Do you need a hand?'

'No, we'll be right,' the doctor said. 'There are three of us plus the priest and his assistants.'

The good Catholic in Frank was coming out. The village had a strong Catholic emphasis with its church and school. He immediately started fooling around with the kids. I stayed near the helicopter and with the help of the crewmen, let people have a look inside. We were always wary of any unwanted presents that they may choose to leave behind.

The numbers just kept growing as word of the medical team travelled around the area. So much so that the team ran out of supplies. The doctor decided that we would all go back to Nui Dat and get more. It was only a few minutes away. The area was not secure enough to leave some behind working while we did a resupply run.

We were back in less than an hour and the crowd had swelled even more.

'I managed to grab some barley sugar while I was back in camp,' the doctor said. 'Would you like to give it out as they come over to the helicopter?'

'Sure,' Frank said. 'We can use it as a reward if they do as they are told.'

Ulcerated sores and malaria were the main problems. There were a few more serious cases that the doc arranged to receive further treatment. One of our helicopters tended to be on this community service run most Sundays for quite a while.

The next day I teamed up with Laddie.

'They want us to spray the Task Force for mosquitoes. I did a bit of spraying in New Guinea and it's real messy,' he said.

'What are we going to use?' I asked. 'We don't have any spray gear.'

'If we put a tube into the drum and stick the other end out into the slipstream it will siphon out and spray around,' he said. Luckily, before we departed the ground crew were able to organise a spray outfit from the American supply area.

'They've found a set-up the yanks have used. Let's go and have a look at it.'

The ground crew and one of the gunners, Jim had fitted the unit. There was a big plastic container in the back of the helicopter and a spray bar across under the cabin above the skids. The container was full of liquid, which sloshed around as we flew up to Nui Dat.

'War against mosquitoes', RAAF News, December 1966.

'OK, here goes,' Laddie said. 'Turn on the spray.'

We did a couple of runs and the container was empty.

'They have more on Kangaroo Pad; let's top up.'

After several runs and top-ups they ran out of insecticide. It seemed to be using a lot more than planned.

'Can you keep the spray on and come back tomorrow,' the engineer asked.

'Should be able to,' Laddie responded. 'I only think we need one more run.'

'I'll arrange insecticide from back beach to be brought over and you can load at Vung Tau.'

'How about we fly over to back beach and load there.'

'That's even better,' the engineer responded. 'See you tomorrow.'

Unfortunately, a few days after we sprayed the leaves started falling off the rubber trees. It appeared that the container had been used for defoliant on its previous job and it hadn't been cleaned out completely. The small amount of residue was powerful enough to cause the leaves to die. While we may have reduced the number of mosquitoes, we also exposed everyone in headquarters to the elements for the next few months as the leaves regrew.

***

The publicity about the helicopter involvement in the Battle of Long Tan brought a journalist named Geoffrey Murray AAP, to the squadron to do a story. I was 'chosen' to be his guide. He started with a picture of Pete, a World War II and Korean War fighter pilot, the oldest in the squadron with me, the Academy graduate and youngest. This appeared as the associated picture. As we flew around carrying out routine sorties on Kangaroo Standby, I gave him a running dialogue on how the army would be lost without us. My contention was that our support provided them with a much more comfortable and less demanding war.

When the article appeared in *The Sun* newspaper in Melbourne, the headline read 'Helicopter pilot says army would be lost without us'. My dad's boss, a brigadier, lived next door. So, before breakfast there was this call across the fence.

'Keith, you seen the newspaper yet?'

'Just the front page. What's up?'

'What have you been teaching that son of yours?' he said as he passed the paper folded in the middle.

'Typical,' he mumbled. 'Trust him not to think before he speaks.'

'Those air force types don't realise they wouldn't have a job without us.'

'Got it too easy.'

And so, I once again put my poor old man on the spot. The context was lost on a couple of old diggers who didn't appreciate that I was talking about the new soldier and his support system.

Good times in the Boozer, Cliff and Tony.

Back at Villa Anna they had built a new mess for us in the yard where we could all gather for a drink. It was a prefabricated tin shed with a concrete floor, a few refrigerators, a bench for a bar and several outdoor chairs with a couple of tables. We didn't mind, it had a cosiness we enjoyed. Occasionally a passer-by would throw a rock on the roof. We were trained not to rush outside, even if it turned out to be a grenade. A VC tactic was to have an anti-personnel mine set outside to get you all as you rushed out. These infrequent moments were always a little disturbing. Usually resolved by another drink. Our original gathering point became a recreation area and the centre for our slot-car racing track for some time.

***

Operation Vaucluse began on 8 September in the Nui Dinh hills to the west of the Task Force area and overlooking Route 15 to Saigon. We did a helicopter insertion of 6RAR and withdrew 5RAR at the end of their Operation Toledo from the same pad to the east of the mountains. It was only 9 kilometres from the Task Force and it became a continuous stream of helicopters taking off and landing between the two locations. We flew at treetop level across relatively flat and jungle-covered countryside. Although there was the potential for enemy troops to fire on us, our exposure was very limited to any jungle location and we rarely flew over the same path twice. With five or six trips each and four fully kitted soldiers per trip, we placed a company on the ground in just over half an hour.

The next day I did an SAS insertion with Frank. It was still very wet everywhere from the monsoon rains. We flared into the clearing following Max's instructions from above.

'We're picking up a lot of spray from the grass, Frank,' Bluey said.

'Looks like a bit of water. They'll need to disembark from a hover.'

'Hovering now,' Frank called. 'Tell them to jump.'

'The first guy has disappeared. No there he is. The water must be nearly 2 metres deep. They have their rifles above their heads. The water is up to one guy's neck!' Bluey gave us a running commentary.

'They'll survive,' Frank said as he pulled pitch. 'Let's get out of here.'

No-one wanted to hang around in the area we dropped the SAS patrols as it was deep in enemy territory. It also could compromise the patrol as they attempted to arrive undetected.

I was on Kangaroo Standby for the next nine days. Other crews were assigned to resupply tasks with the battalion out on the operation. This task could become very tedious as we waited around much of the day for a task, which often only took 15 to 20 minutes. We all had different ways of whiling away the time. Most read books between games of cards. A small fire was usually set and a brew was always available. A waiting area was finally organised with a tent, table and a few chairs. As long as the weather was fine it was OK. Unfortunately, we couldn't wander away from the helicopters as we were on immediate readiness standby.

***

Our tasks were usually very routine: flying between 1ALSG at Vung Tau and Nui Dat with minor supplies and spare parts; an odd trip to the provincial headquarters at Baria with intelligence officers; taking R&R troops to Vung Tau and returning with 'refreshed' troops; and leaflet drops out to the eastern side of the province as we continued to encourage VC to change sides.

Bruce and I did a SAS insertion to the north of the Nui Dinh hills. These missions usually only took a total of 15 minutes. On a trip like this we took off from Nui Dat and headed in a direction towards a small clearing in the jungle that placed the patrol as close as possible to their target area for reconnaissance. Flying at treetop height you wove between and around the taller canopy tops dropping down as you passed over cleared areas. The lead helicopter above gave directions as it was difficult to navigate at such a low level and across featureless terrain.

It was quite exciting, required close watch for any obstacles like dead branches sticking out, and was tinged with the uncertainty that at any time you may pass over the enemy and receive ground-fire. On this trip as we wove between the trees a large monkey suddenly came into view swinging between the trees. It conjured up the cartoon image of the monkey spreadeagled across our windscreen, looking at us with surprise on his face. We missed him.

The lead helicopter continually provided fine tuning for the direction to fly and the distance to run. It was a hectic five to ten minutes. You flared, landed and departed, all in a few seconds. The trip back home always felt less stressful. We placed the patrol in suspected enemy locations and they hid there watching for any movement. In this case they were looking for retreating enemy from the operation in the Nui Dinh mountain range. They were collected a few days later. On some other occasions the patrol would be discovered and a 'hot' extraction was required as they were withdrawn with the enemy pursuing them.

I switched to being on logistic support of the operation from 17 to 20 September. This involved two to three hours flying each day as we took out supplies, repositioned troops, returned rubbish and carried messengers from one position to another. I averaged 20 sorties, which equated to 20 jobs each day.

I was flying back to Vung Tau with Frank after a leaflet drop when we heard a mayday call on the emergency frequency. These were a regular occurrence over the radio emergency frequency. Often it was fighters over North Vietnam talking to radar warning aircraft as they tried to avoid ground to air missiles. It was always a reminder that the air war was not as docile as it appeared in Phuoc Tuy Province. However, on this occasion it was in our area.

'That's just west of here,' Frank said. 'Albatross 19 is in the area; time on task 3 minutes,' he radioed.

'That puts it in the Nui Dinhs,' I said after I checked the map. 'He must have been supporting Operation Vaucluse.'

'I see some smoke rising from the hill, about three clicks slightly to our right,' Bluey said from the back.

'I've got it,' responded Frank.

As we flew towards it you could see that the fighter bomber had not made it over the crest of the hill and wreckage was strewn along the ridge line.

The #2 was circling the area. 'I saw a parachute deploy,' he said. 'Can you see him anywhere?'

'I'll fly back down the line of the crash,' Frank said. 'Keep your eyes open for the parachute or the pilot. Also keep a lookout for Charlie; he's known to be in this area.'

'There's a parachute swinging in the trees, Frank,' Blue said. 'Two-o'clock 500 metres.'

I can't see anyone in it.

'We'll need to put someone on the ground to look around,' Frank said. 'Is there anywhere to land?'

'Crusader 2 we have found a parachute, no sign of the pilot.'

'No clearing in the immediate area.'

'Albatross 19 this is Sunray 91, we are less than 1000 metres to the east. We will dispatch a search party.'

'Roger 91, Albatross 19 we will hold to the east in case you need us.'

'Better they wander around that jungle than me,' Blue said.

The body of the pilot was found in the jungle near the parachute. He had failed to pull up early enough from his bombing run in support of 6RAR and clipped the ridge line. While his ejection seat blew him clear of the aircraft he broke from the harness on impact as he plummeted into the treetops without sufficient height for the parachute canopy to deploy properly. The troops on the ground took his body to an area where a US Dust-off aircraft, which had scrambled to the call from Saigon, picked it up.

'Children ride in helicopters', RAAF News, December 1966.

Following a few more days on Kangaroo Courier I had a day off. By this time more recreational equipment had arrived. One item was a sailboard. It had a retractable centre board and a 12-foot (3.6-metre) mast. I took it out with just a mainsail, but when someone came with me we added the jib. It was fun to sail out among the ships at anchor off the beach. Most of my expeditions were without incident, although I remember once when a wind storm blew up out of nowhere. Bill G one of the ex-RAF pilots, and I had to make a downwind run in front of it to get home. The sailboard was never too stable and with two big fellas on board it was worse, making for a fast and scary ride.

We were always looking for opportunities to win the hearts and minds of the locals. I remember that late in the month it was decided to do a public relations exercise and take people from Hoa Long for a ride in a helicopter. There was no doubt that the boys enjoyed it, although the older folk were a bit apprehensive.

To end the month Dave and I were on the Dust-off Standby at Nui Data. There were several non-emergency call outs and we brought the sick and injured back to the Aid Post. We also took one digger with a viral infection of some sort to the hospital at Vung Tau.

So September ended with another 50 hours flying.

***

I had a day off early in October and Big Black had come down from Nui Dat for a break as well. He again got us a huge supply of ammunition and we went to the rifle range. We both enjoyed firing weapons and rationalised that it was good training in case we came face to face with the enemy. He brought an M60 machine gun with him on this occasion. The belts had tracer loaded and so we were able to play making lines in the sky with our bursts. We gradually extended the range of the targets we were firing at and could see the huge arc that the bullets followed as they covered the distance. It was fascinating to 'walk' the arc in onto the target. Suddenly the barrel started to smoke.

'Shit!' said Black, 'We've cooked the barrel.'

We struggled to disengage it without burning our hands. It finally came away and we laughed our heads off. I then challenged him to a pistol competition in which we would throw Coke cans in the air behind the other's back and the shooter had to spin around and see if he could hit the can. The one who hit the most cans with one magazine was the winner. I managed to hit the can just before it hit the ground, but had used up most of my magazine. Black took his time and took fewer bullets to hit it each time.

He had also brought a grenade launcher. We fired them over several hundred metres and it was interesting to watch the slow-moving grenade arc towards the target.

After returning the weapons to the armoury we went downtown for a drink at one of the beach-side bars. These were just a trestle table plus a couple of stools with an ice box from which a young girl or boy served drinks. Not that these drinking spots were always safe. On one occasion a claymore mine was exploded that killed three US soldiers as they sat at the bar.

It turned out to be a jealous boyfriend, concerned at how much attention they were paying to his girl.

Big Black stayed overnight at Villa Anna. An indication of the different stresses that people like Black, who lived up at Nui Dat, were under came during the night. We were awoken to the sound of yelling and screaming. Black was fighting with his mosquito net and yelling. He was having a nightmare.

'I've got him. Don't let the bastard get away. Grab him he's trying to kill me. That will teach you, you little bastard.'

The army had its own flight of Bell Sioux reconnaissance helicopters. They provided forward observation for commanders planning operations and general light support. They were based at Nui Dat as they were under the direct command of the brigadier. Their compliance and performance was often used by him as he continued to argue for the Iroquois to be moved to the Task Force area. However, during my time in Vietnam they had a higher rate of unserviceability and more frequent accidents. Bruce and I went up to Binh Gia to take ground support personnel for one Sioux early in October that had suffered an engine failure. They were unable to fix it and a Chinook was called in to lift it back to Vung Tau.

On the way home we joined others at Hoa Long where we gave the children rides in the helicopter as another part of the 'winning hearts and minds' program.

***

Operation Canberra started on 6 October, and on the next day Laddie and I were tasked to the battalion. First thing we took the CO 5RAR on a reconnaissance to Dat Do and took one VC prisoner back to Nui Dat. Our task was then to take supplies to Charlie and Delta Companies of 5RAR as they set up to secure Route 15 to Saigon. We flew a total of 40 sorties between Nui Dat and 5RAR.

On the next day I flew with our CO as we did an extraction of an SAS patrol from the Nui Thai Vai Mountains in the south-east of the province where they had been checking on the movements of VC troops who could attack 5RAR. That they were in the area was confirmed that afternoon as Dave and I were sent in on a medivac for four of our diggers who had been wounded by mine booby traps.

Still later in the day we went back and extracted the remaining members of that platoon.

We continued to resupply 5RAR in the morning of the next day. During this work we noted that a flight of American B52s out of

Thailand were dropping bombs just to our north to disrupt VC emplacements. Suddenly we were called to change task and pick up a group of officers to fly to the village of Phu My near the bombing area. As we approached the village it was obvious that the pattern of bombs had fallen a little to the west of where it was intended.

A 'carpet' of bombs from a group of B52s clears the area where they land and replaces it with a 'moonscape' of craters. The carpet had hit the edge of the village and destroyed about five homes. Reports were sent back to Saigon of the damage. We did not land as it was not regarded as an appropriate time, nor were we the right people, to start consoling the villagers. Later a construction party went to the village and assisted the villagers to reconstruct their houses and roads.

In the afternoon we assisted in the withdrawal of 5RAR back to Nui Dat. Before going home, we inserted a SAS patrol into the area for further reconnaissance and finally arrived home after dark.

Occasionally we got to fly out of the province. On 11 October, Cliff and I did a couple of courier runs between Vung Tau and Nui Dat before a flight to Bien Hoa and back with a logistics officer from 1ALSG to collect some supplies. While the terrain was not dissimilar in this area to the north of Phuoc Tuy, the increased number of roads and traffic, and the incredible size of the US military bases were always an eye opener.

For the next three days I was on Kangaroo Standby and courier duties. This proved to be fairly quiet as the battalions were not out on operations, just routine clearing patrols within line Alpha. This line only extended out to enemy mortar range.

Bruce, Dave, Cliff and I decided to go to the American Officers' Club for dinner one evening around this time. We had a few drinks and listened to the music. Before we knew it, it was curfew time.

'Will we stay here for the night?' Bruce asked.

'No, let's make a run for it,' Dave said.

It was only two blocks back to our villa. We had a jeep and I was driving.

'OK,' I said, 'We'd be unlucky to get caught.'

We jumped into the jeep and I drove out the gate and turned right towards Villa Anna. A set of headlights came on behind us.

'Looks like the MPs,' Dave said, 'Gun it, Bob! If we're lucky the gate will still be open and we can get away.'

I pushed the accelerator to the floor and the jeep charged down the street. We hit a bump in the road and everyone nearly flew out. I came to the villa and spun into the drive. The gate was shut. The MP's jeep pulled up behind us.

'Can I see your ID card, sir?' the tall African-American MP said in a southern drawl.

'You should know better, sir,' he said as he took my details, got back in the jeep and drove away.

The guards let us in and we went off to bed wondering what, if anything would happen. I did not have to wait long. The next morning, I was called into the CO's office, given a dressing down and placed on a week's orderly officer duty. So, I got to drive a jeep back and forth to the airstrip instead of flying for the next week. I guess I was lucky not to be charged.

When I got back into the air, Operation Queanbeyan was in full swing back in the Nui Thai Vai hills again. Unfortunately, Cliff had had a major accident on 18 October. He was lifting out of a pad with dynamite on board and as he reached the treetops the helicopter plunged back into the trees. A fire started in the engine area at the back of the cabin. Cliff was able to crawl away with a badly injured back. One crewman was injured, but was also able to drag himself away.

The copilot, Pete, was trapped in his seat by a tree between his legs. The other crewman, Gordon, came to his aid. He tried to pull him out through the back of the seat, but his back started to catch fire as the fire behind him started to take hold. So, he went to the front and tore the damaged perspex away and managed to get Pete out through the front around the tree. He dragged him away as the helicopter was engulfed in flames. Gordon received the George Medal, the highest award for valour while not under enemy fire. Cliff and Pete were sent on a medivac home to Australia. An old mate, Les, arrived as Cliff's replacement.

'Helicopter hero', The Sun, 15 Feb 1967.

***

During these operational times we had a lot of flying resupplying the troops in the field, taking out reinforcements, returning sick soldiers and repositioning groups within the area of operation. After the operation concluded on 26 October we returned to routine courier and standby duties.

October was a very busy month and despite not flying for one week I did 64 hours flying and 451 sorties. Apart from my enforced time off, I had only two days off flying for the month.

The next operation was to be into two of the islands in the delta of the river system to Saigon. They were just to the west of our road between Vung Tau and Nui Dat and south of the beginning of Route 15 to Saigon. It was suspected that they were staging posts for supplies to the VC. A battalion clearing operation, called Operation Hayman, was to be carried out by 5RAR.

My first task was to fly over the islands dropping leaflets. This warned the population that we were coming and asked them to cooperate. Our next task was to lift the battalion onto the island of Long Son and then to fly all the civilians off the island. This was quite a task. Most had never been in anything like a helicopter before and, of course, they were not sure where or why we were taking them. We flew 357 civilians to Ba Ria for screening and flew them back later.

Our orders were to take as many as we could on each load. This became a juggle between how many we could physically fit on the floor in the back and how much they weighed. We rarely had a weight problem. It became a competition to see who could get the largest number on board. The winner had 19 Vietnamese women and children on board. It was a bit like 'how many can you get into a phone booth?', or 'how many bodies can you fit into a Volkswagen?' Remember, we were only able to carry four fully kitted soldiers.

We continued to support this operation every day until 12 October. The squadron's support this time was particularly important as there were no other means of movement across the creeks and swamps.

Dave and I took 6RAR personnel on reconnaissance flights on the 17th as they prepared for Operation Ingham. This took place to the east of the Task Force area, halfway to Xuyen Moc. The topography in this area was relatively flat areas of jungle with very few villages. It was generally regarded that this was a hostile region and extreme caution was needed. In conjunction with this operation we inserted a series of SAS patrols into an area further north east as forward reconnaissance.

Our standby moved to the 6RAR Eagle Farm Pad and we carried out regular trips to the forward positions. Often we would take meals from the battalion kitchen as a break from the hard rations that the troops carried. Once again these would be in thermos boxes and were usually steak and vegetables plus ice-cream as dessert. Certainly a nourishing break and another mission that helped us win the hearts of the soldiers.

'Helicopters clash with Viet Cong', RAAF News, December 1966.

Returning to Vung Tau on 17 October I heard a mayday call. The position was just to our west and so I turned towards the location. It was a South Vietnamese Air Force A1 ground attack plane. The wingman was circling the area. It was in the flat, muddy delta area south of Route 15 and we couldn't see any crash site as we flew around.

'Look out for any signs of a parachute and the pilot,' I said, 'We might be able to pick him up.'

'There's some papers in the water down below,' Brian the crewman replied.

'Let's hover over it, see if you can pick them up.'

'Lower, boss, lower, pass me that hook,' Brian said. Our skids were touching the water. 'I've got them; it's a map.'

'I can see a heat haze ahead,' I said. It had appeared in my reference point as I was hovering. 'You right to move forward?'

'Roger.'

'I can see a small fire on the surface and a piece of metal. What do you think it is?'

'All that churned mud means he has gone in vertically,' Frank said. 'The poor bugger has been buried already.'

We reported our findings and headed on home.

By the end of the month I had done 72 hours flying and 457 sorties, my busiest month so far.

***

Operation Ingham continued until 3 December. I flew with the CO on this day as we extracted the battalion back to Nui Dat.

Scotty was a man of very few words who professionally and methodically carried out his tasks. This carried over to me as I attempted to not make any mistakes or blunder through any of the radio procedures.

On the next day, the first of two operations began guarding Route 15 for the movement of American reinforcements and resupplies into Vietnam through Vung Tau. Once again, the magnitude of the convoys and the amount of equipment that was involved overwhelmed the senses. Our troop deployment and support was generally by road so we played little part. We did provide an airborne command centre that gave our commander an expansive view. Most of the squadron's activity involved Kangaroo Standby and courier runs.

On 5 December, an airstrip called Luscombe Field was opened at Nui Dat. This allowed resupplies to be flown directly into the area using larger aircraft than the helicopter; for instance, the Caribou.

I was given the job to do a Father Christmas run on 25 December. We flew around some of the local villages distributing sweets. (I did another Christmas flight the next year from Butterworth in Malaysia. I flew a Dakota DC3 that was all decorated in Christmas fare to Vung Tau and we brought eight stretcher patients back to the RAAF hospital in Malaysia as a special surprise. Normally they would have had to wait for the next Hercules C130 to take them away from the war zone. I had a medical team on board that looked after the patients. They thoroughly enjoyed this day as we lumbered home.) Similarly, the children in the villages were excited yet bemused by the sight of Father Christmas as he appeared bearing gifts.

The SAS continued their activity over the Christmas-New Year period; after all there could hardly be holidays during war time, and I did three routine insertions and extractions into different locations within the province. We were always on the lookout for significant movement of enemy troops, perhaps indicating a planned attack.

One of my most hair-raising experiences occurred during this time. The squadron did a troop extraction on 28 December and I was flying the larger D model that we got after Cliff's crash. It could take a bigger payload but had a larger rotor diameter and was heavier. All this meant that it had more momentum than the B model and you needed to have more anticipation in your actions. The CO decided to use the regular line astern pattern, with each of us following the other as we snaked down into the pad, landing a few seconds apart.

I was put at the tail of the line with the bigger helicopter. As we dived down the CO tightened the turn back into the pad using a tail rotor turn and I was 'whipped' off the end due to the greater momentum of the D model. When I kicked the pedal to do a similar turn, my helicopter just kept going. I went 'sliding' down under the other helicopters and out the other side. It gave Les a great introduction to how 'hairy' things can become. Remember, we were approaching treetop level before I went under the other helicopters!

At the end of the month Dave and I took a training team member down into the Mekong Delta region. This was a fascinating journey, firstly because I had not been this far away or in this southern region before and because of the nature of the landscape. There were a multitude of creeks and channels with all the surrounding countryside also appearing to be under water. Boats of all shapes and sizes plied the waters, their size depending upon the size of the waterway. Villages appeared to be of stick and straw huts all perched on stilts.

Everyone we saw was up to their knees in mud. Underlying this landscape was the knowledge that this was not a friendly area and that we needed to be on the lookout at all times for any signs of enemy fire at our helicopter.

Any innocent-looking sampan could be under the control of an angry VC with a weapon that he could fire and hide again in the blink of an eye.

Due to the decrease in requirement for our support December only involved 47 hours flying for me. Significantly, as the New Year emerged I knew that half my time in the country had passed. It was also the time when the squadron would start changing over the crews and create a stagger so that there would always be pilots with in country experience to initiate and mentor the new arrivals.

TRYING TO MAKE A DIFFERENCE

For the next 15 years of my life I felt that I was in a position to make a difference. I did change a significant number of young people's lives, but I continued to feel unfulfilled. My ability to perceive the hidden agendas of higher authorities may have been clouded by my determination to focus on the needs of students and a dogged blindness to my fallibility. Years of independent thought and relative isolation from my peers provided a platform for vulnerability.

When I arrived at St Barnabas' School to be interviewed for the role of principal there was no doubt in my mind that it was the job for me. The farm school was run down and needed a total reconstitution of its buildings, focus and image. It catered for unsettled adolescents. It was my type of environment and challenge. I got the job after the initial choice, an agriculture teacher, decided that it was not really the location or status that would set him on his pathway to leadership. I accepted the challenge and was not perturbed by the five-year time line I was given by the School Council to achieve a major turnaround for the school.

The school was on 100 acres (40 hectares), had an operating commercial dairy and a market garden that had the potential to provide many of the needs for the kitchen. While the school had less than 70 potential students for the following year, predominantly of Aboriginal and Islander descent, I believed that it had the potential to provide a place for a growing number of students who weren't thriving a in traditional school setting. Over the next five years the numbers grew to over 200 students and the school was serving the special needs of students from Darwin to Melbourne.

We had an innovative education program that provided the students with a university entrance score, while also focussing on adventure, vocational skills and self-worth. My philosophy was that the students may not have had an academic focus, but if they chose to change their degree of application they had an opportunity for further study. After a few years the approach bore fruit and several students were able to enrol in diploma courses of an agricultural nature. For others the involvement in more academic subjects gained them favourable job placements.

I expanded outdoor education to include canoeing, rafting, abseiling and horse riding. The latter became so successful that we needed to lease more land. Our horse instructor's popularity grew and as we trained more and more horses for local stations our own herd of horses grew to 80. A measure of success was when 24 students prepared a horse each, along with all associated equipment, to participate in the very challenging bicentennial horse ride from Maytown to Cooktown for ten days along the old gold route.

Students were attracted to the school's non-traditional program. Many were referred by social workers or court attendants as a last opportunity to avoid penal institutions. I gathered a suitably qualified staff to show these young people how they could develop skills that would enhance their potential. Together with a small group of teachers they worked to help each individual find a focus for their life. Not that this was a simple process. Many had come from significantly disadvantaged environments where academic achievement and/or work stability were not a natural situation. We had both boys and girls, which required settling many boyfriend/girlfriend feuds-not to mention attempting to minimise sexual promiscuity. Most of the kids wanted to settle disputes through physical intimidation.

Attempting to beat the system was a natural discourse. I feel I called upon the skills of survival in Vietnam, which involved knowledge of my craft, intelligence on the intentions of the opposition and guile to do the unexpected in achieving outcomes. Consequently, for example, it was not uncommon for me to camouflage myself in dark clothing and move around the campus in the dark observing what was going on; to sit up in trees observing unacceptable activity, such as drinking alcohol; to step out of the bushes and intercept a resupply run from the local hotel; or, to put putty over screws on the screens of the girls' dormitory to recognise when an unauthorised entry had taken place.

But perhaps most significantly, it was my non-traditional approach to the use of all this knowledge that helped me most. Rather than penalise the offenders, say with exclusion from the school, I would share my knowledge, illustrate how easy it was for me to be able to be informed and then work cooperatively towards better solutions and decision making. This developed a trust and openness of communication through which it was possible to work towards changed values.

Our unconventional approach attracted the focus of the *60 Minutes* crew while they were in North Queensland. As Jana Wendt said, 'What is a liberal like you doing out here in the bush?' The students answered for me when they told her that it was the first school they wanted to stay at or had not been kicked out of. The town rallied around us in support, asking that the program not focus on the negative 'fringe' interpretations by conservative elements but on the good it was doing. The program did not go to air. But the damage was done.

Th conservative church hierarchy, using economic rationalist decision making, moved to close down the school and sell the property. While I was devastated that the church could not see the value in the school's activities, I was not in a position to argue and the five years had already been extended. I was emotionally stretched by the experience and recognised the need to recharge and find a similar challenge elsewhere.

I moved to a sister school in Cairns and taught mathematics. During the year an opportunity arose. This time the school was closer to civilisation, being in Warwick on the Darling Downs, and again it was catering for mainly Aboriginal and Islander students and only had a current enrolment of 70. I was determined to learn from my mistakes, but equally determined to still focus on the needs of the students. I expanded the academic opportunity, but focused on self-determination and self-direction in the organisation of the curriculum through a contract-based approach. To support my endeavour, I enrolled in a Doctor of Education program, which allowed me to provide an academic rigorous study of the value of the approach.

I again built enrolments up to 200 over a few years, increasing the number of Warwick town students and adding a group of international students from predominantly Asian countries. I was criticised again by more conservative elements for the liberal and non-traditional approach. However, I had established international recognition of the school, created a sound academic foundation for the approach and looked forward to expanding enrolments.

Once again economic rationalists provided the bullets with which the church could argue that the school had an unsustainable future. There were five secondary schools in a small city of 10,000 people and none had the potential to become large enough according to the statisticians. Despite an outcry from the local community, the facilities of the school were put up for sale.

Many argued that I was ahead of my time and that society was not ready in the mid-nineties for the empowerment of students. I saw it as an institution more concerned with its bureaucracy and status than the educational needs of a group of young people. Maybe the others were right as we now see the thrust of new programs for middle schooling focussing on student-centred issues with delivery of the curriculum that we were using.

I chose not to move to another school. I had been running boarding schools for the past 13 years that had involved 24-hour, 7-day-a-week supervision. I had a vision for the future of education and hoped to ignite the excitement of change in educational leaders through consultancy. I soon found the resistance to change is strong and if you are not going to say what they want to hear people are not prepared to listen. My world began to crumble around me.

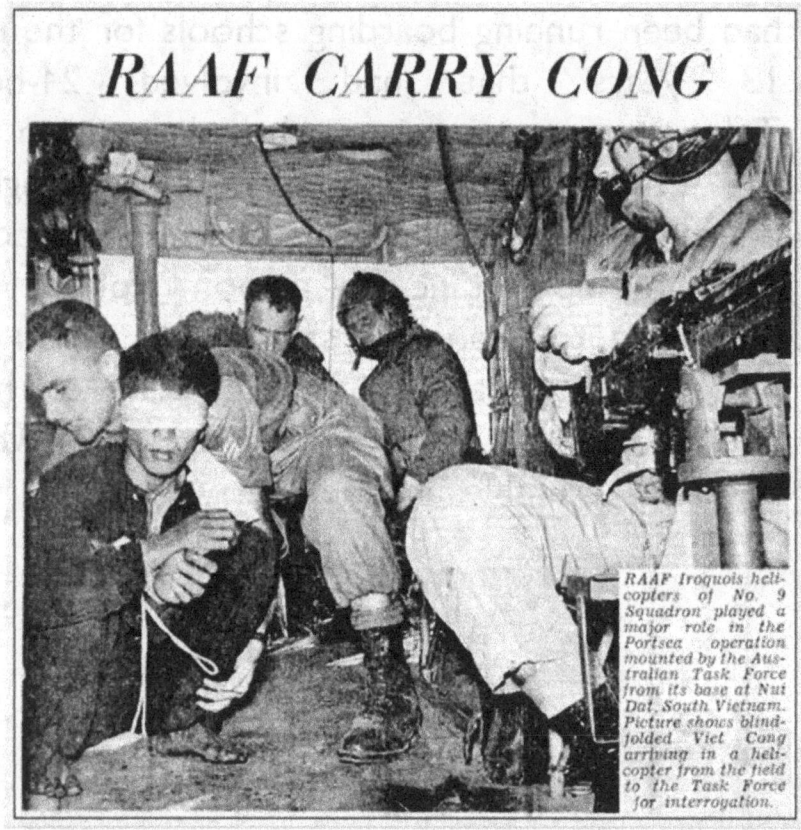

'RAAF Carry Cong', The Australian, 8 April 1967.

CHAPTER 6

STARTING THE CHANGEOVER

January to March 1967

In January people started to move home at regular intervals to either Australia or Malaysia. The roster was announced and I had the dubious pleasure of being the last to go home, Consequently, I was the only one of the original group to do a full 12 months. Laddie said it was because I was the youngest and could handle it-I think I just drew the short straw, again.

Apart from those injured the first to go was the CO. To my chagrin, the new CO was my old adversary from the RAAF Academy and someone with whom I did not have a great rapport. I knew that my next six months would be a little rocky. Unfortunately, my briefing with the new boss laid the groundwork.

'Now, Bob, I know we have had our differences in the past. But I am looking to you for leadership in the squadron. We will let bygones be bygones. There are a few things that I hope I will not see.' And off he went on a tirade of criticism, listing things he didn't like about me. Obviously, I said, 'No, sir; yes, sir; no, sir. Things will be fine, sir,' all the time thinking, 'Why did this have to happen to me?'

Our intrepid leader showed his colours after his first walk to breakfast. It was a couple of hundred metres down the street to the dining hall. However, the culture of the region was to slip out to the edge of the road just before dawn and excrete on the edge of the bitumen. There was no sewerage and the theory was that the rain would wash the roads clean. Consequently, there were little piles of fresh, often 'baby shit yellow' poo along the road that had to be traversed. The CO drove his jeep to breakfast every day from then on, rather than accept the challenge.

On New Year's Day, Les and I participated in an airborne assault. There was always an air of excitement during these operations as we flew low over the jungle canopy, weaving left and right between treetops and along valleys. We knew that the plan was to get as close to 'Charlie' as possible and surprise him with the attack. Because we so rarely came into contact with the enemy, the troops were keen for a chance to 'get amongst them'. As we flared over the landing spot, the troops were almost out of the aircraft before we had landed.

Each departure made the helicopter lighter and it tended to spring back into the air. Coordinating the positive contact with the ground, bottoming the collective and disembarking the troops, all within a few seconds, was always one of the challenges in an airborne assault. They rushed into the jungle fringe, picking up formations and consolidating the potential of those already there. They were gone out of sight almost as fast as we departed the landing zone (LZ). Les and I then sat around Nui Dat for the rest of the day on Dust-off Standby in case the assault made contact and there were casualties.

The periods between involvements in operations were very mundane and as I have said before, just like being a courier van running messages and personnel here and there. An occasional emergency broke the routine. We received a call for a medivac of a wounded VC one night. I went with Max and we flew to Nui Dat.

It was very black flying up along the road with no traffic, lights or navigational aids to guide you. Towns did not have a lot of light associated with them, although Ba Ria, as a large town, stood out. At Nui Dat headlights were used to guide us to the spot where a group of soldiers were waiting. They carried out the wounded enemy soldier on a stretcher with a two-man armed guard. We flew him to the hospital in Vung Tau.

I flew back and forward between Vung Tau and Saigon three times on 7 January, twice on the 10th and twice on the 12th. It seemed that there was no coordination between those wanting to go there for different meetings or visits. Maybe in quiet times trips to this bustling city seemed like a good idea. Our squadron managed to get some training in during these quiet times. I did gunnery training for the crewmen and some practice hoisting. This came in handy because on 11 January I was called in to winch a wounded ARVN soldier out of the jungle and take him to hospital in Ba Ria.

As part of new control measures on the movement of the civilian population there were 'No Go' areas promulgated. We would fly over these areas on the way back to Vung Tau and chase anyone out of them. We had the authority to kill if we thought there was any threat to us or other elements of the Australian forces. In general, it was people trying to get back to their crops and harvest them. Unfortunately, they often supplied part of their load to the Viet Cong, either willingly or unwillingly. This was why we were trying to control the movement.

On one of these missions there was a cart being pulled by a buffalo and another guy on a bike moving towards the edge of the prohibited area away from Long Tan village. We decided to give the intruders a 'hurry up' and frighten them from entering again. As we opened up with machine gun fire behind them the buffalo broke into a gallop and they looked just like a cartoon, with the guy on the cart flying into the air at the end of the reins and goods falling off the cart as they bumped down the track. The man on the bicycle started pedalling at a furious rate and passed the buffalo cart. It was funny to watch, but in fact we were worried that we had made the wrong decision and would be chastised for not killing them. This was a part of the conundrum that we faced, with ill-defined friend or foe and no clear boundaries to areas occupied by the enemy. There was a stray cow in the area, which we decided must have been a VC cow and we killed it as our first kill in Vietnam.

On another occasion a small boy was herding a group of cattle towards the prohibited area. We flew down and stampeded the cattle away from the direction he was heading them. I recall looking down and seeing him waving his fist in the air at us. While we may have felt that we were doing a humane thing, he obviously had other ideas. This conflict between helping the people of South Vietnam and interfering with their way of life was always complicated.

Towards the middle of the month I was on Dust-off Standby with Dave in the Task Force area in a properly equipped helicopter, including a winch. A call came over the radio for help from a South Vietnamese Army Company who were part of the current operation. As I was preparing to leave our recently arrived new CO responded to the call, saying he was in the area. But he was in a larger model helicopter with a wider rotor width and without a winch. Despite advice to the contrary, he continued into the small clearing to evacuate the wounded. His rotors chopped into several trees, cutting them off. He managed to get back out of the pad and take the wounded to the nearby ARVN hospital in Baria. As he was heading home to Vung Tau the helicopter was suffering extensive vibration from the damaged rotor. The blades had to be replaced before it could fly again.

That night in the bar the CO tried to justify his humanitarian actions to me.

'I was in the area so it was the right thing to do wasn't it, Bob?' he asked.

'I'll have a beer, Terry,' I said as I tried to ignore him.

'I looked down and saw the wounded soldiers and just had to get in.'

'You're bloody lucky you didn't cause a disaster,' I retorted.

'What do you mean?'

'Well, to go in and try to be a hero was a foolish decision, given I was a couple of minutes away with a helicopter with a winch on. After all, you were in a Delta model. They're bigger you know!'

'There's no need to get sarcastic.'

'The call was for a winch evacuation,' I said as I tried to control my frustration.

'But it looked like I could make it,' he said. 'We did get in.'

'Look at the damage you did to the rotors. What would have happened if one had given way?'

'That wouldn't happen.'

'What if you had lost control and crashed into the pad with the wounded and their support team?' Which was really close to what actually happened as the momentum of the bigger helicopter took over.

'But, I did the right thing didn't I, saving those guys?'

'You fucked up, sir,' I said as my frustration let go. 'You fucked up! We all have a job to do and it's teamwork. We all don't try to be heroes, sir.'

'I guess I shouldn't have expected any more from you,' he said as he turned indignantly away. Then why did you ask, I thought as I walked over to Dave and Cliff to enjoy my drink. I guess this form of response had a lot to do with the long-running battle between us over many years. I certainly wasn't going to support his call for a medal for himself.

A hot extraction that certainly was heroic was carried out by Max on 18 January, which he later recounted to us in the bar. It was for the first SAS soldier to be wounded on patrol by a VC ambush. Despite their best efforts the rest of the patrol realised that they could not move him as they remained under fire from the enemy. They formed a defensive perimeter around him. A distress call went out and a helicopter extraction team went to their aid. It became obvious that the soldiers would have to be winched out of the jungle.

Two factors made this extremely difficult and dangerous. Firstly, the winch travelled at 80 feet per minute (25 metres per minute) and the canopy was at least this height. There would be at least two minutes as the winch went down and back up again! When you consider that there were four men, the helicopter would have to hover at the top of the canopy for at least ten minutes. Secondly, the enemy were in the jungle below in significant numbers, firing at the soldiers and then the helicopter. Despite all this, Max held his helicopter in a hover while all four were safely winched up. The supporting fire of the door gunners from both helicopters and from two gunships helped to interfere with the potential of the VC to bring accurate fire to bear on the hovering helicopter.

It must be recognised that the door gunner on the right had to operate the winch so there was no firing from the side on which the pilot sat in the hovering helicopter. The gunners reported that they had numerous targets to fire at as the VC moved around in the jungle below. This extraction was one in which the tremendous firepower of the helicopter gunship was realised and fully utilised. The fire discipline of the SAS must also be commended as they held their position on the ground with one man down. Max was awarded a DFC for this tremendous effort.

I had to endure the joy of flying with the CO on two days as we did a reconnaissance into an area in which we could do an airborne assault the next day with 6RAR These proved to be very quiet times with limited chatter between the crew. I always felt that he was looking for affirmation of his ideas, something I was rarely willing to provide.

However, I was not to participate any further in this operation as I went off on R&R. There were several places that we were able to go, some by choice and others by designation. Hong

Kong and Manila were the favoured places. Bangkok was my allotted destination. Our pilots from Butterworth in Malaysia felt lucky as they went home for the five-day break. Later, Australia became a destination and some people were able to go home for their break. Those who chose to go back to Australia had the difficult problem of leaving the family to return to Vietnam with the real fear and haunting possibility of never returning. To experience this on one occasion was enough for most people.

I flew to Saigon on a C123 courier and then boarded a Pan American 707 to Bangkok. Everyone was excited about escaping the war for a brief period and generally the opportunity to stay intoxicated for five days. I was the only air force person and there were two Australian diggers on the flight. The rest were Americans. We arrived and were allocated a hotel. On arrival, about the middle of the day, we asked where the nearest bar was and went to get a drink of Singha beer. The bars were slightly more upmarket than Vung Tau with better music, more dancing go-go girls and bigger bars. They operated continuously and were full of R&R servicemen.

That evening I contacted some close friends of my father who I had known as I was growing up and arranged to go to dinner the next night.

We went out to another bar in the evening, where we drank to the sound of 'canned' music and I did a lot of people watching. The guys disappeared, and I nodded off in a taxi home.

The next day I headed out to the big US Forces BX that I had heard a lot about. My wife had given me instructions about some things I should buy. I bought a lot of Canon towels and sheets. That evening when I was discussing over dinner what I had been doing with Betty, the wife of an Australian Army friend of my father who was stationed in Bangkok, she bought it all from me (as they could not shop there even though they were Australian Service Personnel) and I had to go back to buy it again. Unfortunately for Jan, the same range of goods was not available the next day. I went out for a meal and listened to more music again that next night. Throughout the night I was propositioned with a wide range of exotic opportunities. However, as soon as the girls realised that I was not going to take them home they became disinterested in my company. This was their livelihood and they were not going to waste time on a cheap Australian.

Then it was the last effective day and I went shopping for a black star sapphire to take home to Jan. I bought a tear-drop-shaped gem from a shop that my friends had recommended but was never sure how good it was. I ate Thai food as I wandered around, and found it very tasty, although one often wondered about the conditions in which it was prepared. But I had a cast-iron constitution and I wanted to try things. The city was obviously overcrowded, and it was fascinating to just observe all the different people. The big difference to Vietnam was that the people were happy and laughing, always wanting to make conversation, usually trying to sell you something.

Early the next morning the bus called by the hotel and we commenced the journey back home. The few days passed quickly, and I did not feel that I was all that refreshed. Probably because we had not left Asia and the environment was fundamentally the same, although the number of beers consumed may have been a contributing factor.

The day after my return I teamed up with Les and we moved troops around that were involved in Operation Wollongong. In the afternoon we did an interesting extraction of a SAS patrol. Everything was going as normal as Bruce guided me into the location he had confirmed from above. The patrol was being pursued by VC and we weren't sure if we'd get them out before they arrived. The clearing was an old rice paddy and I put down in a bit of water. The soldiers appeared from the side and jumped aboard. As I was about to pull pitch and fly out straight ahead the water in front of me started to erupt from rifle fire. The VC had arrived and were firing ahead of me so that I would fly into the hail of bullets. Not to be outdone I pulled back on the cyclic column as I pulled pitch on the collective and we flew out of the clearing backwards, quickly rolling onto our side and heading off at treetop level. We must have left the enemy wondering what went wrong.

***

Around this time, I had a visit from a friend who I'd grown up with; his father was in the army too. We both had a day off and he asked me to come downtown with him for a drink.

'When did you arrive in the country?'

'A few weeks ago,' Kerry said. 'I'm a forward observer in artillery.'

'How's it going?'

'Not bad.'

I wasn't convinced.

'Got a letter from my mum last week,' he said as he handed it to me.

'How is she?' I asked as I started to read. The letter was about a news articles that she had read and how terrible it was that we were killing our own with 'friendly fire'.

'What she doesn't know is that it was me,' he said. 'How do I tell her?' 'What do you mean?'

'Well, we were being over-run by the VC and they were only about 50 metres to our front. They were obviously about to charge again, so I ordered fire on a position directly to our front. They got up to charge at the same time as the rounds arrived. It might have stopped them, but shrapnel also ripped through our position. Several guys were wounded and a couple died from their wounds.'

'But your mum's letter talks about a range of incidents, not just that one,' I said.

'Yeah, but what do I tell her?'

'Nothing, mate. Nothing at all. As an army wife she should have known better than to raise that question. Did your father say anything?'

'No. Maybe she wrote this without talking to him.'

'How do you feel about it all?'.

'Well, I had no choice. If I hadn't called it down the VC would have been inside the fire and over-ran us. It was a calculated risk. I often wonder why I didn't get hit. I was right up the front. It's certainly no fun listening to guys around you screaming in agony as the metal rips into them. I don't know what else I could have done.'

'You're not the only one, mate. It's one of those risks we take. Better men than you have stuffed up. Let's have another beer.'

We agreed that there would be no mention to his mother of his involvement while we could still think rationally. We drifted from bar to bar and ended up in the American Officer's Club where we had a meal. Some 38 years later when I next spoke to him he told me that he had rationalised his actions of this day and was able to face up to it. He certainly remembered, somewhat vaguely, that we got drunk together. He was not the first, nor the last, to wrestle with their involvement in calling artillery fire that caused injury and death to our own troops.

***

There were also accidents in the air. After an SAS extraction at the beginning of February the two US gunships were flying back to their base outside Saigon. They were at 2000 feet. Suddenly the second helicopter watched in disbelief as the tail rotor came off the helicopter in front of them, wound around on its drive shaft and entered the main rotor disc. The impact caused the assembly to disintegrate and rip the engine plus the back of the helicopter off. The cabin with the four airmen in it then fell to the ground. The fall would have seemed an eternity to those inside. It was horrific for those watching, who frantically radioed for help and landed to recognise that no-one survived. Our inspections of the 'Jesus nut', as the attachment nut for the tail rotor was called, were extremely thorough.

Around this time the army challenged the air force to a game of Australian Rules football. It was to be played on the Vung Tau soccer field in the centre of town as a public relations activity. The CO heard about it and called me to his office.

'I hear there is a football match; you are not to play.'

'When's that?' I said, playing dumb.

'I don't know. But this is an operational theatre and I don't want any of my pilots injured in silly games.'

'No, sir,' I said, noncommittally. Once again, issues were rising from our relationship in the past.

I found out when the game was on and got Laddie to leave me off the roster. When he asked why, I told him he didn't want to know. Tony, the new equipment officer, and I had been key players and selectors for the air force in the past. The game was a roaring success with many locals astounded at the nature of the game. More importantly we managed to beat the more favoured army team. We went downtown and got one of the locals to strike a set of miniature VFL (Vietnam Football League) Premiership Cups in the image of the famous VFL (Victorian Football League) Cup, which I still have in my cupboard. The next day I was a little sore and sorry, but I managed to hobble around.

'You didn't play in that game yesterday did you, Grandin?' the CO asked.

'Who, me?' I responded and hurried away. The only disappointment was not being able to publicly join Tony as he celebrated our victory in the Officers' Mess.

Task Force operations at this time were close in to Nui Dat. We had limited involvement. I recall a fascinating sight as I was positioning to Nui Dat early one morning with one of the new pilots, Mick, who was just off flying training course. He was only 19 and looked like a schoolboy. He arrived in Vietnam as one of the first pilots direct from Flight Training School. Up till this time all our squadron pilots had previous experience within other RAAF squadrons and many flying hours. The shortage of experienced pilots forced the hierarchy to try using a similar approach to the USA, who sent short commission pilots direct from training to Vietnam service.

As we flew north the dawn was just breaking and everything was quite peaceful and serene. We noted that a flight of B52s were leaving their condensation trails (con trails) in the air as they moved over the country for an early morning bomb run. They were like a flock of geese as they made their arrow pattern in sections of three aircraft. As we watched we saw vertical con trails appear under each aircraft. They were dropping their bombs and the humidity conditions were right for the bombs to form their own con trails. It was raining bombs with lethal long white tails. As they approached the ground the tails disappeared from the bombs. But as they exploded on impact new pressure waves formed their own patterns in the sky. Each was a series of semicircles emanating from where the bomb had exploded. We were too far away to see the flash of the explosion, but these waves gave the same effect as one after the other they appeared and then dissipated as they reached further out from the impact point. It was quite an extraordinary show that took very precise atmospheric conditions for us to be able to see it.

Early in the month I did a dramatic troop repositioning as part of Operation Wollongong. A company of 5RAR had arrived at a ravine about 1 kilometre across in the Nui Dinh range and asked for helicopter assistance in crossing. It would save them a day, which it would have taken to go down and up again. When Ted and I arrived we found that there was no landing area, except for a large rock that we could put one skid on. Our manoeuvre then became remaining at the hover, which involved maintaining power so that the helicopter was in fact still in flying mode, but also putting some pressure on the skid in contact with the rock for stability as the troops jumped in. The other side of the helicopter was suspended in space.

The CSM (company sergeant major) and three troops jumped aboard and we lifted off the rock, sank into the valley to gain forward speed and rose to the other side of the ravine. We found a small clearing and the CSM set about making it bigger. We returned to collect the next four troops. We did this trip 25 times, making 50 sorties in just over an hour and moving 100 troops.

I went with Laddie on a flight to Soc Trang down in the Delta Region a couple of days later. It was to the same junk base that I had gone to with Dave in December. Once again, we were transporting a training team member back to his base of operations. He told us how they camouflaged heavily armed patrol boats as junks and moved up and down the river hoping to be attacked by pirate VC chasing supplies. You can imagine their surprise when they pulled alongside and saw all the armament. Not that it was the type of war I wished to be fighting.

On standby at Nui Dat I bumped into an old school classmate, Fred. In fact, the one who took up with my girlfriend when I went off to the air force. He was an infantry company commander and would be coming to Vietnam with the next battalion. He was at Nui Dat on a forward reconnaissance and general familiarisation trip before embarkation. We arranged to meet before he went back, but circumstances did not allow that to happen.

On 14 February, the next day, I was on medivac standby when a call came in that there had been a mine explosion and three officers of Charlie Company had been killed. As I flew out I realised that Fred was with this group. We landed next to the site of the accident and they rushed the bodies into the back of the helicopter. Foolishly, I looked around to see if Fred was one of them. The bodies were a mass of open wounds with blood, fat and organs 'bubbling' out. I was never to look around again. I could not recognise any features. Luckily, Fred was not one of them. He actually took charge and commanded the withdrawal. The three officers had been in a circle leaning over a map adjacent to a fence, with Fred standing behind them, when they triggered a booby trap.

Above: An ever-ready Iroquois crewman mans a side machine gun as RAAF helicopters formate on the way to a task in the Vietnam delta country.

'Flying over the Delta', RAAF News, November 1966.

I had started to be unwell, with a 'bug' that could not be overpowered or stabilised. Various courses of drugs were not controlling the situation. It was decided that I should be medivaced to Changi Hospital in Singapore. I spent the next six weeks undergoing tests and treatment until they felt that all was stable. I must admit to still having a very sensitive bowel that went 'off without much provocation. I was anxious in hospital as I awaited the outcome of each test; I was bored as I whiled away each day in bed; and frustrated at being out of action with a non-combat-related illness. It was the end of March before I was sent back to the squadron.

While I had been away several of the original members of the squadron had returned home. Operations Bribie and Renmark had also been conducted in the Long Hai hill area with significant casualties to our troops. Even though there had not been a major contact with enemy troops, the activities of the Task Force group had become more confrontational. Our flying was more frequent and could be described as more intense as we penetrated into VC areas they had regarded as safe havens.

THE PAST CLOSES IN

I joined the Association of Independent Schools of Queensland (AISQ) as a consultant and was sponsored to work alongside a professor in the USA for a few months before sharing the learning gained with schools around the state. My enthusiasm was high and the program ground breaking. But I found that the entrenched attitudes and practices of teachers in front of a class were very hard to change. Despite the potential for them to understand each individual student better and for the student to be able to demonstrate what they had learned more clearly, school practice remained focused on traditional testing forms of assessment and comparative scores.

Many teachers recognised that classroom outcomes were often less than desirable and that a change in pedagogy was needed, but it had to be a 'quick fix' to minimise the backlash from administrators and parents during any change. What I had to offer was a fundamental philosophical change that would take time to impact. Enthusiasm quickly waned, even amongst teachers who could see the potential of the concept. I began to seek employment to follow my one-year contract with AISQ, but I failed to gain any interviews. I began to face the prospect of not having a salary for the first time in my life.

In January 1999 we were without any form of income. Like so many, my wife and I looked to small business as a way forward and purchased a small gift shop for my wife to operate with borrowed money. I continued to seek employment and finally registered with Education Queensland as a relief teacher. A few days before school started in February I was offered a one-term contract teaching mathematics. I accepted, hoping that I could help students and possibly the school, but I was soon to recognise the total powerlessness that my position now placed me in. I was directed how, what and at what rate to teach the class, no matter what the ability of the students was or their degree of participation in the learning process. By the end of the term I was a broken man, fearing the prospect of facing the children or even going to work. I withdrew my services from the relief list so I could restore my sense of self-worth.

I helped my wife on a casual relief basis and with the computerised accounting program. But depression began to take a serious hold and I started to spiral downwards. At the time I thought it was just my age and failure to gain a work relationship, but it was also the onset of the depressive impact of my past experiences; in particular, my Vietnam service. When I turned 60 the following year I became eligible for a service pension. We were just surviving financially; our shop was not providing an adequate income so we had to place it on the market.

We had begun the frugal life of living on the pension when suddenly an opportunity to go back and work with the Professor in the USA arose. The position offered was only as research assistant, but we dreamed of a growing potential and consultancy future back in Australia after a few years. In November 2000 I departed for New Jersey.

America was an overwhelming experience. Everything was so big, so hectic and so impersonal that it became an existence rather than a fulfilling time. Having a wage that did not do much more than meet the bills did not help the situation. I felt an internal anger that influenced my relationships. Then the bombing of the Twin Towers on 9/11 occurred.

The impact of this experience was immediate. Around me there was a growing fear and a growing chaos. The university closed down and people rushed home to be with their loved ones during this time of impending threat. I started to act as I had been trained, focused on survival through order rather than panic. I gathered my things and went home to Jan. She had been out on her morning walk and came home to 'unreal' reports on the television.

We moved onto our balcony on the 10th floor of an apartment block that was on a major arterial road and the flight path into Philadelphia. The road was rapidly becoming empty and there were no aircraft in the skies. The quiet was pervasive. As night fell the only movements were the lights of fighter aircraft flying racetrack patterns over the nearby nuclear plants, so they could immediately react to any threat by suicide pilots. It felt like the war zone that it was.

OUR 'COPTERS HIT CONG RIVER BASE

NUI DAT, South Vietnam, Wed., AAP. — Australian "mini-gun" helicopters blasted apart a Viet Cong storage camp area and sampan supply base in Phuoc Tuy Province this week, Air Force officials said today.

The helicopters were from No. 9 Squadron, stationed at Vung Tau, 20 miles south-east of here.

In a surprise raid on the camp on the Rai River east of Nui Dat — which is regularly used by Viet Cong supply boats — the helicopters sank a sampan, set fire to a large enemy rice cache and destroyed shelters and bunkers.

A crew member of one of the two helicopters was winched to the ground after the attack to collect Viet Cong papers scattered around the camp by bullets from the twin machine guns.

"We hovered over area"

The lead attack helicopter was captained by Flt.-Lt. Les Morris, of Canberra, and the second by Flt.-Lt. Bob Grandin, of Melbourne.

Morris said: "We hovered over the area for a few minutes before we picked up the camouflaged position. It turned out to be a rice cache, as we split open the bags with machine gun fire and set them alight with smoke bombs.

"The sampan was hidden under mangroves and we sank that. While we were moving around our blades sent papers studding over the camp. I thought they could have intelligence value and sent a crew member down on a winch to collect them."

Leading Aircraftman Dave Spalding, of Southport, Queensland, was winched down.

"It was a small camp, but well camouflaged," he said. "There was one well fortified bunker so I sprayed that with fire as I moved into the camp itself.

"I found some tinned food, field utensils and the papers which were made."

The Deputy Leader of the A.L.P., Mr Lance Barnard, yesterday visited Australian troops at the Nui Dat base camp.

'Our 'copters hit Cong river base', The Sun, 25 May 1967.

This was followed shortly afterwards by anthrax being included in the mail of prominent people, which had the flow-on effect of potentially contaminating everyone's letters. Warnings were broadcast on television to only open your mail with gloved hands. As people died or became sick, it was very difficult to feel comfortable in an alien environment. It was several days before the aircraft started flying again and traffic started to get back to normal.

America became a paranoid nation that withdrew into itself and seemed focused on magnanimous platitudes. I found that I had moved into a defensive frame of mind and was thinking like I was in a war zone where I needed to have my wits about me and have escape plans for a wide range of occurrences. Being so far away from my family became a stress in my life. I missed the familiarity and colour of home. I found it difficult to understand the growing anger and frustration within me, so I decided that I needed to cut my time short and return home.

CHAPTER 7

COUNTDOWN

April to June 1967

I was back in action on 4 April and the next two months were the busiest I spent in Vietnam. I had 71 days to go and so, as per tradition, I got a 100-day countdown chart and started to colour a section each day. As you can imagine, the chart was of the female form. These charts were a US service invention called a FYGMO chart-an anagram for fuck you, got my orders. The body was similar to a colour by numbers painting with the biggest numbers-and first to colour-starting at the extremities.

Wherever you went these charts could be seen, often on the wall behind a workstation desk. They were items of comradeship, conversation and sometimes envy. After nine long months it provided a lift in spirits as a physical view of the diminishing days could be seen. It also conjured up images of warmth that had been missing for so long.

A major activity that had commenced during my absence was the building of a mined fence in the south-east between Dat Do and the coast.

This was designed to interfere with the supply routes from the coast into the centre of the province. We now had an aircraft on standby in Vung Tau as it was closer to the operations on the fence. My first week back was on this standby.

The fence was a contentious tactic. Many people were concerned that the enemy would steal mines and use them against us. They also became good at moving the mines so that when we were moving along pathways that we thought were safe we would tread on a mine. During the early phase, the soldiers were using regular intervals between posts. But when they set off a mine at the place for a new post it was recognised that the enemy had worked this out and booby trapped the position. When the team arrived next day for further work they often found that the enemy had herded cattle or pigs through the fence to set off the mines for them. The rising number of mine casualties caused most of the argument.

Our task was to fly supplies from the stores depot at the back beach to the troops at the fence line. On one such trip I had unloaded stores and was about to depart when there was a loud explosion close by. I saw a soldier falling back down to earth only 20 metres away after being thrown into the air by a mine. I moved the helicopter closer, without thinking about the mines around me. They ran with him to the helicopter and we took off straight away for the hospital at Vung Tau. He was very blue, but one soldier worked away at CPR and kept him alive. Others tied tourniquets to his injured limbs. We were at the hospital in just over five minutes and this helped save his life.

I did another medivac at night with Dave after a day on Vung Tau standby. It was a call from US forces operating with ARVN troops in the east of Phuoc Tuy near Xuyen Moc. We flew out across a black landscape with no sign of lights. We used our direction finder to get a bearing from their radio transmission and flew along this line searching for the torch light they said they were shining upwards. While it's hard to believe you could find one light in such a landscape, once you are in the vicinity it becomes quite clear. It's just getting into the vicinity. Following a contact which had wounded two of the soldiers, the enemy were also obviously still in the vicinity. We could not use our landing lights.

'I have the torch,' called Bluey from the back. 'Two o'clock 300 metres.'

'Roger that,' replied Dave. 'Prepare the winch.'

'Albatross have you overhead,' called the patrol. 'Have been able to clear an area; you should be able to land.'

'Roger,' I replied.

'Watch the tail in the back,' Dave said. 'We'll go down slowly and see how clear it is.'

'Small tree about 7:30; rotate 20 degrees right,' Brian called from his side.

'All clear right,' responded Bluey.

'We're getting pretty close to the canopy on the left,' I told Dave.

'Do you think we can get down, Blue?' Dave asked.

'Yeah, you have about 3 metres on the right.'

'That's it, no stumps below,' called Brian.

As soon as we settled members of the patrol rushed forward with two stretchers. We slid them in the back and started lift-off as soon as they retreated.

'Move a bit left,' Bluey said. 'We're under the overhang.'

'OK, approaching the canopy now. Clear to rotate?' Dave asked.

'Roger, clear both sides.'

We headed off back to the American hospital on the back beach at Vung Tau. They had a 24-hour casualty team that rushed out with their wheeled stretchers and whisked the wounded into a waiting operating theatre. We headed back to our landing pad and into Villa Anna for a quiet drink before retiring.

A few days later I was flying with Bill G, one of the Poms who had recently arrived in the country. Back home my young wife had the dubious pleasure of teaching his wife, Betty, an absent-minded middle-aged English woman, to drive for the first time, something Jan had been telling me about in her letters. Bill G and I were working as a pair with Dave and Geoff B. Our task was to bring a patrol back that had been operating to the north-west of the Task Force Area. I went in first and collected four of the patrol. Then Dave went in and picked up the other four while I circled overhead. As he pulled pitch and started to rise out of the pad there was a large flame out of the exhaust.

'Shit, did you see that?'

'He's gone back in. I'm going back to pick them up,' I said.

As I descended I noticed that his troops had disembarked and were setting up a defensive perimeter.

'Tell the guys that we're going to drop them off and they're to defend the helicopter while we get help. Bill, radio base and tell them 19 has had an engine failure. Give them the coordinates.'

'Watch the tail for me. I think I can squeeze in,' I said as I watched both the still rotating blade of Dave's helicopter and the trees on the right.

'That rotor is fucking close, boss,' Bluey said.

'Yeah, but it's missing,' I said as I watched the two tips passing each other about 15 centimetres apart. 'How are those trees behind us?'

'Clear.'

We touched down and the troops disembarked and formed a perimeter. Dave rushed over to my window.

'How about I take your crew to Binh Ba?'

He waved to his guys and they ran over and jumped in. The crewmen bought their M60s from the mountings on the side of the helicopter and the ammunition bins. I pulled pitch and the overpitching alarm started to squeal. This told us that the load was too heavy. I couldn't lift them all. Dave leaned forward.

'The crewmen are going to stay with the troops. You can come back and get them.'

'OK, let's go.'

We lifted up and flew the short distance to the ARVN garrison at Binh Ba. I dropped Dave and Geoff B then flew back for the crewmen. This time they had tethered the other rotor so there was more space. I took the crewmen back to Binh Ba. By this time another helicopter had arrived from the squadron with Laddie on board.

'I'll go in first and pick up half the patrol,' I suggested on the radio.

'Negative on that. The area's too small. We'll arrange a sapper group to clear some trees. Then we can also try to pick up the helicopter. The troops can stay and guard the helicopter.'

I flew back to Binh Ba and picked up the crew to take them to Vung Tau. I was able to use the airstrip to do a running take-off with the heavy load. Later that day a Chinook helicopter lifted 19 up and took it back to base. It was discovered that the operations in very dusty conditions had caused a build-up on the inlet guide vanes to the jet engine. This created disturbed airflow that reduced the fatigue life of blades in the first row of the axial compressor. As soon as one sheared off it flew back into the engine causing catastrophic failure. All engines were changed at 500 hours instead of the normal 1000 hours operation as a precaution against a recurrence of this failure.

Later in the month I flew with Frank to Saigon to pick up the RAAF officer commanding our forces in Vietnam who had recently arrived in the country and was to visit Vung Tau and the Task Force. As usual there were aircraft everywhere.

'Keep a good lookout,' Frank said.

It seemed no sooner had he said it than I urgently called, 'It looks like a couple of exhaust trails heading our way at 9 o' clock.'

A quick look and Frank realised that they were at our height, closing fast. He bunted the helicopter and dived towards the ground. The poor air commodore was thrown off his seat and into the cockpit between us. Just then there was an incredibly loud noise as two Phantom fighter bombers blasted past just above us.

'Sorry, sir, welcome to Vietnam,' Frank said with a laugh.

Bluey and I were doing a compass swing, after an engine change on one of our helicopters, in the corner of the aerodrome the next day when a distress call was received for a medivac. Someone had fallen and badly hurt their back at ALSG just over the sandhills. I was told to go and airlift him to hospital without waiting for another pilot. They felt it would be smoother, and quicker, than by road as they were concerned he had broken his back. With the impact of helicopter vibration on pilots' backs, I wasn't too sure about the wisdom of the decision.

Pictures from Vietnam', RAAF News, November 1966.

The next day I got looked in the eye of an angry VC who wanted to shoot me. Bill G and I were doing a hot extraction of a SAS patrol.

'Let's get out of here quick,' Bill G said as he put down in the jungle pad.

The SAS were firing into the jungle as they ran backwards towards the helicopter.

'Permission to provide covering fire, skip?' came from the back.

'Roger, keep it above their heads.'

'There's one at 11 o'clock,' I yelled. He had stood up from behind a log about 15 metres away and pointed his rifle my way. Adrenaline rushed through my veins at the horrific thought that I was a helpless sitting duck. My job was to follow through on the controls in case Bill G got shot.

'Got him,' yelled Bluey as he swung his M60 onto the target with a continuous burst of fire. The VC disappeared behind the log. Bill G was pulling pitch and we were heading off through the trees.

'Targets on the left side of the pad,' I called to the supporting gunships that strafed the area.

'Shit that was close,' I said. My whole body was drained as my heart continued to beat rapidly. 'Did you get him, Blue?'

'Don't know, but sure as shit gave him a fright.'

The next day I was flying with Bill G again and we took part in the movement of the newly arrived 7RAR on Operation Puckapunyal. Once again, they went into the area around the Nui Nghe mountain range to the north-west. By the end of the month I had done 57 hours flying and 330 sorties.

Laddie illustrated the increased determination to meet the needs of the army. He was asked to do an extra job at the end of the day. He determined that he had enough fuel to complete the job and get home, just. As he was approaching Vung Tau after completing the task he suddenly ran out of fuel. He made a perfect autorotation onto the bank of one of the mangrove creeks just off the end of the runway. A Chinook helicopter was called to lift him home. Unfortunately, the delay in its arrival allowed the tide to come in and enter the bottom of the helicopter. Subsequent testing indicated that the fuel gauge was over-reading by about six minutes, a time within which Laddie could have completed the mission safely.

***

As May began I had 45 days to go. Two arms and a leg were completed on my FYGMO chart. At this time we were involved in Operation Lismore, inserting 7RAR in conjunction with two companies of US Army Aviation helicopters. We were in the midst of masses of helicopters landing troops into a large cleared area. While there was security in numbers for the ground troops in this type of assault, we worried about so many helicopters being such a big target; whether the enemy gained intelligence on this action and mined the clearing; or whether they were in the jungle waiting to rain mortar bombs down on us. We also worried that not everyone knew the routine and that there would be mid-air collisions.

After dropping my troops I was called to divert to an accident site, where a mine had exploded under an APC. As we approached the road near the accident engineers were waving mine detectors around to check that the area was clear. Beside the road was an APC on its side with broken tracks. Troops were clearing all the gear out of it. Another group was moving towards the road with a couple of stretchers. We were given the signal that it was clear to land. We collected two wounded and flew them back to Vung Tau.

A few days later we repeated the mass helicopter exercise, but this time we were withdrawing the battalion. At least this time we knew the clearing was secure, although you never knew if the VC were near enough to fire some mortars into the field.

The simple depth of danger that you could face in Vung Tau was highlighted one day. A drunken US soldier on his way down the road came across a QC (Vietnamese policeman) wheeling his bike along. He decided he would like a ride and tried to convey his request to the QC. Despite resistance the soldier pulled the bike away and rode around in circles on the road. The QC decided he was a threat, drew his gun, blew his whistle and when the soldier continued to ride in circles he shot him dead. The law stated that if anyone did not respond after the police blew their whistle they could be shot. This action made us very wary of Vietnamese police officers and even made us wonder which side they were on.

Kangaroo and Vung Tau standby filled each day as I continued to count down the days. On one I was flying with a replacement pilot called Trevor. We had had an interesting conversation the night before. I woke to see him sitting by the window looking out.

'G'day, Trev, how's it going, mate?' I asked.

'OK, just not getting to sleep.'

'Why's that?'

'I'm worried we'll be attacked as we sleep.'

'But there's guards.'

'Yeah, but there was a shot last night. That means someone's coming over the wall.'

'It also means someone's awake and alert, Trev,' I said as I tried to help.

'But what if he misses him? They could sneak in and cut our throats,' he responded.

'That's their job and there are plenty of them.'

'I can't sleep. I need to keep watch.'

'But the fact that there was a shot means someone is awake and protecting you. You can't stay awake forever, mate.'

'I know. I feel absolutely buggered. I haven't slept since I got here.'

'Well, you go to sleep and I will watch for you.'

He lay down and was off to sleep quickly. I passed the conversation on to Laddie as Trev was an old buddy of his.

With 28 days to go I was involved in a hot SAS extraction that started with an ominous premonition. Both arms and legs plus the face were now coloured in on my chart.

We arrived at Nui Dat helicopter pad in Phuoc Tuy Province at about 3.30 in the afternoon. It was another tropical day; hot with no sign of rain as it was the dry season. I was leading another insertion of a SAS patrol behind enemy lines with Thommo as my copilot. We were not expecting any difficulties with this task as operations had been quiet for some time. But you can never be sure. Mick was flying #2.

Soon after we closed down the SAS patrol of four emerged from the rubber plantation that was Task Force headquarters. It always amazed me how these guys could disappear into the jungle amongst the enemy and lie hidden for three or four days collecting intelligence information on the movement of the VC forces. Then they would emerge again for us to collect and return to base. They were certainly dressed for the part, their camouflage blending into the shadows of the surroundings.

They carried huge packs on their backs and a wide variety of pouches strapped around their person. Several of these carried extra magazines of ammunition to complement the two magazines taped together upside down to each other that were in their rifle. They were quiet and tense. No last-minute cigarettes for them. They had stopped smoking a few days before the operation so there would not be any smell of Western tobacco on their breath. They had also been eating Vietnamese food for the last few days for the same reason. They sat down in the shade to the side of the pad.

Their leader moved towards me stealthily. He introduced himself as Steve. We stood together using the back floor of the helicopter as a table for his map. He confirmed the small clearing in the jungle on his pictomap. These maps were a photographic image of the jungle and were enhanced to show tracks, huts and waterways. I confirmed that I had the same location marked on my map. We discussed radio frequencies and call signs. We were Albatross 1 and 2; he was Groper 1.

'I'm a bit worried,' Steve said. 'The last couple of times our boys have dropped into the jungle they have been ambushed. Just after the choppers leave. This might just be a bloody coincidence. We do try and drop into their location. But I have a gut feeling they are starting to get smart. They know the gunships are around with the drop and don't want to tangle with them. They are waiting long enough for them to piss off, then they attack.'

'I could hang around a bit,' I said. 'I'll slip over behind the hill on Route 2. It'll only take a couple of minutes to get the slick and gunships back to pick you up. How long?'

'Ten minutes will do. Just long enough for them to think you guys have gone,' Steve said. 'I might be getting paranoid. After all, I'm on "short time" and I want to make it home. We've been here nearly a year now. I feel they're starting to wake up to how we do things.'

'No worries. I've only got a month to go too, so I know how you feel.'

He went back to his squad and I moved over to brief the crews. We were waiting for the gunships to arrive; it was typical for these guys to be late. The demands for gunship support were high and so they were always very busy. You often wondered how they felt when nothing happened during a task. Most of them lived for a fight and relished being able to unleash all their weapons onto a target. But you didn't go without them; they made all the difference if things turned ugly.

We heard them coming. You could always tell the difference. They were so heavy with ammunition that the sound they made had this dull thump to it. As they came around the corner you could see the pilots working flat out to stop their machines. They could not bring them to the hover at the beginning of a mission because they were too heavy. Gunships usually did running landings and take-offs. They skidded across the weldmesh that had been laid over the dirt to give it some stability, coming to a stop in a looping fashion. The directional control rotor struggled to have effect at slow speed.

Unlike our slick ships, which were camouflaged and had dull identification marks, these helicopters were highly decorated with rattle-snakes, each with a mouth that terminated at the barrel of a canon or grenade launcher. The pilots were also flamboyantly dressed, looking more like World War II fighter pilots than modern professionals. But they were good at their job, daring to turn and fight when others only wanted to run. The leader sidled over with his map and checked the grid reference of the drop point.

'We're Rattler 1 and 2. Will we shut down, or can we get going?' he said.

'We can go straight away,' I responded. 'But the guys want us to hang around a bit afterwards. Is that possible for you?'

'How long? We have another job straight after this at Binh Bah.'

'About ten minutes should do it.'

'OK, but let's get going.' He headed back to his gunship, sticking his head into the window of Rattler 2 to confirm what was going on.

I waved my hands in a circling motion to signal 'let's go'. The SAS climbed into Albatross 2 as I departed towards the drop point. I was almost there when I heard the others call leaving Nui Dat. The clearing was big enough. It was covered in thick grass and there were no signs of enemy movement in the area. The clearing reminded me of that time during the wet when we dropped a patrol which disappeared up to their necks in water that was hidden under the tall grass. I turned towards Route 2 and saw the other three helicopters heading up the road. I called to them that I had them visual and told them to turn left.

'Roll out now, 2000 metres to go,' I radioed.

Mick was at treetop level, weaving slightly every so often to miss higher tree canopies. The two gunships trailed him by a couple of hundred metres, sitting a little higher as they did not manoeuvre so well at their weight.

'Albatross 2, left a bit. That's it. Standby to flare,' I called as I helped him aim for the clearing, which of course he could not see.

'Albatross 2, flare now. Watch the small tree on the left.'

I watched as Mick flared, touched and departed. The SAS disappeared into the tall grass. The gunships passed down each side with no sign of the enemy to fire at. I turned towards the small hill on Route 2, while the others flew directly back towards Nui Dat. I checked the time on my watch; it was 4.35.

'We'll just fly in a circle around here. Keep your eyes open though. There have been a couple of ambushes on this road over the last two weeks.' I was down low so that the hill would help disperse the sound of the helicopter and make it less likely the VC would know we were still around.

'Ten minutes is up, boss,' said Thommo.

'Let's give it a couple more minutes,' I replied. But I was aware the gunships needed to move on so I called on the radio, 'Rattler 1, this is Albatross 1, all quiet here. Feel free to move on to your next job.'

'Roger. See you again soon. Rattler 1 out.'

No sooner had the transmission finished than the emergency beacon squeal sounded. The adrenaline started to flow. This was the time when you moved into automatic. Your training kept you focused on your role and responsibilities, pushing the fear into the background.

'This is Groper 1, under attack. Request extraction from the same location as soon as possible.'

'Rattler 1, cancel release. Squad under enemy fire. Will carry out hot extraction. Albatross 2, head back north-east. Groper 1, wilco, estimated time of extraction three minutes. I will call for a marker panel as we approach to indicate your exact position.'

'Albatross 2 on my way.'

'Rattler 1 we are 2 kilometres north of Nui Dat. Do you want us to fly direct to the fire-fight or pick up the slick?'

'Roger, Rattler, turn left and pick up the slick. It is about 1 click behind you. Escort the slick into the pick-up zone.'

I had climbed back to 2000 feet and was now over the clearing. It was hard to see anything in the tall grass. There was an occasional puff of smoke as a grenade or larger weapon went off. The door gunners asked to provide supporting fire. I refused as we did not know the exact location of our troops and the others were approaching fast. I called for identification and an iridescent orange panel appeared on the grass in the same location as we had dropped the four SAS. It was to the left of the centre of the clearing. I turned towards the south.

'Albatross 2, turn 20 degrees right, about 30 seconds to go. The squad is in the left middle where you left them, red panel shows their spot. Rattler, friendlies in the left centre of the clearing. Albatross 2, stand by to flare, flare now,' I called as I rattled off the directions to coordinate the extraction.

'Rattler 2, take the left side. Lay some heavy fire onto the edges of the clearing,' called Rattler 1.

'Roger that,' came from Rattler 2. 'I see fire coming from the front edge of the clearing. I will take that out.'

As I looked down, I could see Mick landing in the middle of the clearing. Both his door gunners were firing as the SAS climbed onto the skids. Mick was on his way as they continued to scramble inside. There was lots of tracer fire coming from the gunships and puffs of smoke as they fired grenades. The two gunships were laying down a huge amount of fire. You could see some fire rising from the ground. It passed by the two helicopters as they flew towards the clearing.

You could imagine the sight of the serpents on the sides of the gunships spitting out their lethal venom as they swooped in towards the enemy on the ground. After they flew over the clearing they each swept outwards in a circle to come back again side-by-side for another pass. They continued to follow this process., calling new targets to each other as they drew more and more fire.

'Albatross 2, any problems?'

'No worries. All OK. No damage. Heading to Nui Dat,' replied Mick.

I called Operations at Task Force Headquarters. 'Albatross I has just completed hot extraction with Groper 1. Rattler 1 and 2 laying down fire but are now departing.'

'Roger, Albatross 1. Were there any casualties?'

'Negative. All extracted and OK.'

'Roger, Albatross 1. We plan an artillery mission; can you hold and redirect fire?'

'Roger that, I will hold over Route 2,' I responded. Let's get out of the road, I thought as I was on a line between the Task Force artillery and the clearing. We returned to our holding position near the hill but remained at height this time. We chatted excitedly in the chopper about what we had seen down below. After a short while large plumes of smoke appeared in the jungle.

'Drop 1000.' Smoke appeared again just north of the clearing.

'Drop 100.' Plumes of smoke appeared on both sides of the clearing.

'That's it. You are straddling the clearing.' Not too professional, but I hadn't done any training in redirecting artillery fire. We then flew back to Nui Dat.

The other crew and the SAS patrol were waiting at the pad. They were having a smoke this time. As we shut down, Steve walked over, a big grin on his face.

'I'm stuffed if I know whether they knew we were coming or we just landed in the middle of their camp. No sooner had you gone and we regrouped to move off than we walked into a mob of VC. It was on. I was carrying a M79 grenade launcher. This Charlie stood up in front of me and I just pulled the trigger. Poor bugger he went all to pieces. Couldn't stand the pace, I guess,' he said with a sense of black humour. 'But then it was on. They were everywhere. Luckily, the tall grass gave us cover. We were able to regroup and hide back in the middle of the drop zone. Thanks for getting back so quickly. It was only a matter of time before they flushed us out.'

'No worries. Glad you had that premonition. It helped us to be there sooner.'

'Geeze, those gunships wreak havoc don't they?' he went on. He was still obviously shocked by the experience.

'They sure do,' I replied. 'They're great to have along in this sort of situation. My guess is that together with the artillery they'll have made a mess of that camp. Your guys all OK?'

'Yeah, no sweat.'

'I guess you don't have to go out again for a while?'

'No, that area has been compromised,' he said. 'We get slid down the order for our next task. Anyway, thanks again. We're off to the boozer. See ya.'

Mick came over. 'How was that, mate? Did you see any enemy fire?'

'I was too busy to see anything,' he said. 'Coming out of the flare I saw the panel. Then one of the SAS. I was worried that I would land on one of them. Then I saw them and put down. At that time the whole jungle to the side of me erupted as the gunships let go. It scared the shit out of me. I just pulled pitch and bolted straight ahead. When the gunships started their turn I did one too. I headed back home as fast as I could. It's amazing that you don't get drilled full of holes. I guess they are worried about their own skins as those gunships come swooping in.'

'Welcome to your Vietnam initiation,' I said. 'I've been here for 11 months and haven't had a hit yet. It's hard to know if they are rotten shots or it's our hit-and-run tactics. They don't get a chance to line us up. Anyway, a great effort, mate, well done.'

'I'm bloody glad it's over,' Mick said. 'I hope that doesn't happen too often.'

It was getting dark now. We checked in with operations and were cleared to return to Vung Tau. We did the ten-minute return flight home in the dark.

Sometime later the news came through that Mick was awarded a Distinguished Flying Cross (DFC) for his flying in this extraction. The papers back home were full of the story of the inexperienced pilot's baptism under fire and his courageous effort in saving the patrol.

A few days later I was in action again. One of the Army Sioux helicopters reported sighting a suspected VC supply area. I was flying with Al, who had just arrived in the country, and Les was flying the other helicopter. We were tasked to have a look and destroy anything we found. This was an unusual operation for us, but is indicative of the changing approach. It was in an area to the east, which was regarded as a dangerous area due to high levels of VC activity. We flew low up the river system, keeping a sharp lookout.

'There's a boat under those bushes to our right; we've just passed it,' reported Dennis from the back.

'Watch out for a boat under cover on the right bank, Les. You can start on it and I'll circle back for a go.' Between us we destroyed the sampan.

'There's a raised platform on the other side of the river with something stacked on it,' reported Bluey.

'I'll make a pass on it,' called Les.

As we came back we could see papers had been uncovered by the machine gun fire.

'I'm going to lower someone down and get those papers. Cover me,' Les radioed. He hovered over it and lowered Bluey down to gather what he could. Some of it blew away, but Bluey grabbed what he could, still suspended from the winch.

'It's rice and maps,' Les reported. 'Let's try to destroy the platform.'

'Should we use all our ammo, boss?' Dennis asked.

'No, save some in case we get into other trouble.'

After a few runs there was rice everywhere and the platform had a tilt on it.

'Let's go home, guys. I'll radio the position and they can hit the area with artillery.'

I now had only 23 days to go and I didn't want too much more excitement. Luckily, the work was routine, despite being busy in support of the troops each day. I flew 86 hours and 590 sorties in May, which became my busiest month.

***

I only flew once in June, on the 2nd. I was showing my old instructor Athol the ropes. We had just taken off from Kangaroo Pad on our way back to Vung Tau. As I came around the corner past the Engineers Wombat Pad an Army Sioux helicopter crashed in front of me. I landed beside it as the rotor continued to flop around and fuel was spilling everywhere. They had hit a rice paddy dyke and tipped forward, breaking the perspex bubble.

'Hurry up and get them out in case it catches fire,' I commanded.

The engineering officer was able to walk assisted, but the pilot had to be carried. We moved away a bit out of danger and I turned to see that the pilot was an old mate from my childhood. He had banged up his knees.

'What a bastard of a thing to happen' was all Hutch could mutter.

'Where do you want to go, mate?' I asked.

'Take me back to our area,' he said.

'The engineer wants to be dropped off at his pad. But he says Hutch should go to hospital.'

By the time we had dropped the engineer off Hutch was suffering. We got him to agree to go to the hospital at Vung Tau.

'Give you time to get your story straight, mate,' I suggested.

I was not put on operations for the last ten days. My FYGMO chart was down to the erogenous spots. I had completed 3441 sorties in 546 flying hours.

I am finding it hard to remember how I got home from Vietnam.

I know that I met my wife at RAAF Fairbairn in Canberra, but what aircraft or how we proceeded from one place to another is a mystery. The whole concept of being home was surreal. I remember feelings of uneasiness, of incompleteness and a strange sense of being lost. While I loved the opportunity to be back with my wife and family, I wondered what I had achieved and who cared anyway.

EPILOGUE

The next few years after my US experience became progressively more difficult for me emotionally. I tried to do some relief teaching again to help the family finances. But at the end of each day's endeavour I felt psychologically drained, had a hopeless sense of powerlessness and became more aggressive and abrupt in my relationships. The skills I had had for dealing with disruptive adolescents were suppressed.

I tried to rationalise this by thinking that possibly the rapidly changing nature of society and the interests of 21st century youth had undermined the foundations of my approach, which focused on them individually accepting responsibility for action and shaping a future direction. But I couldn't shift the depressive feelings within me. I started to do less and less relief work, until I stopped altogether in the middle of 2002. But my moodiness remained and I began sinking even lower. Relationships at home were strained.

After a year I decided to try again. Following a seven-day contract I was so emotionally wound up that I had an emotional breakdown, which included verbally attacking my family. This outburst made me recognise that I had a problem. Prior to this time, I lived in a state of denial that there was anything wrong with me. Subsequent visits to a psychiatrist uncovered the underlying stress disorder that almost certainly dated as far back as my war service. A cloud lifted as I recognised the relationship between my emotions, actions and sense of wellbeing.

An application for greater support from the DVA (Department of Veteran's Affairs) was not a simple recognition by them of the relationship between my now diagnosed post-traumatic stress disorder (PTSD) and not working. It took more than two years of battling through review and appeal processes to achieve recognition. Each challenge to my integrity was accompanied by deep depression and a period of rebuilding my self-esteem. During these times I did almost nothing, other than pass through the days.

I faced a future in which I would probably have mood swings. Any work that I did was in 'bursts' or 'flurries' of activity. Despite a real desire to work consistently, I often found that I couldn't force myself to focus. I enrolled in a Bachelor of Arts in Communication to help me have a disciplined approach to work and to improve my writing skills. Writing this discourse became a part of the course and a part of the healing process.

I was also able to do some teaching of Education students at the university. This led me back into working with unsettled students and onto an International Study of the Mental Health of School Students, especially those who were being excluded from schools, which also led me to do another Bachelor of Arts in Psychology. The intensity with which I was working helped me to avoid depression. As one psychiatrist said during my battles with DVA: 'he has an insatiable appetite for work that hides his true feelings'. Consequently, as soon as I finished this degree I enrolled in a Doctor of Philosophy to study the Crisis in Traditional Schooling so that I still had a focus. My future will be in writing, I hope, to keep a continuous sense of purpose.

My deep sense of self-reliance means that I believe that it is my responsibility to work out the issues. I believe I will overcome the barriers that appear in front of me, but I also recognise that denial is a strong emotion during these times. I focus on one battle at a time and I am reviewing this book of my experience that I wrote ten years ago as we approach the fiftieth anniversary of going to Vietnam. What's next?

MORE GREAT READS

Available now online or at all good bookstores

View sample pages, reviews and more information on this and other titles at www.bigskypublishing.com.au

"Vietnam was tough. Most of us were young. We were in a foreign country fighting for a way of life we had barely experienced ourselves. Though the Vietnam War officially ended in 1975, there has been no end to the war for me..."

My Vietnam is Dave Morgan's story. A typical 20 year old, he was forced into extraordinary circumstances in Vietnam.

Far from his carefree youth, the Vietnam War would expose Dave to an atmosphere of ever-present danger and sheer terror that would impact him forever. His return to a divided Australia would isolate him further.

During his service Dave wrote home to his mother from Vietnam tracking the days and the events. In 1992, after his mother passed away, he found all of his letters carefully numbered and in order. He has combined these letters with his own recollections and diary entries, and the short stories of seven other veterans, to capture the unbelievable danger and horror that these young men experienced in Vietnam.

Dave also describes how Vietnam established life-long feelings of intense loyalty, trust and mateship between the men that served there. Dave's story focuses on his time as a soldier and his return psychologically exhausted to a divided nation.

After Vietnam and the freedom of 'home', Dave tried to live a normal life, however the horror he'd experienced caught up with him. The pressure was immense. Eventually, something had to give. It wasn't ever a matter of if, but when you would crack. The impact of Vietnam on his life has been, and continues to be, immeasurable.

'Vietnam picked off the vulnerable like a hungry predator.' Many of those who go to war and survive are scarred forever. My Vietnam is the biography-a coming of age story-of a self confessed ordinary bloke who has lead anything but an ordinary life.

Available now online or at all good bookstores

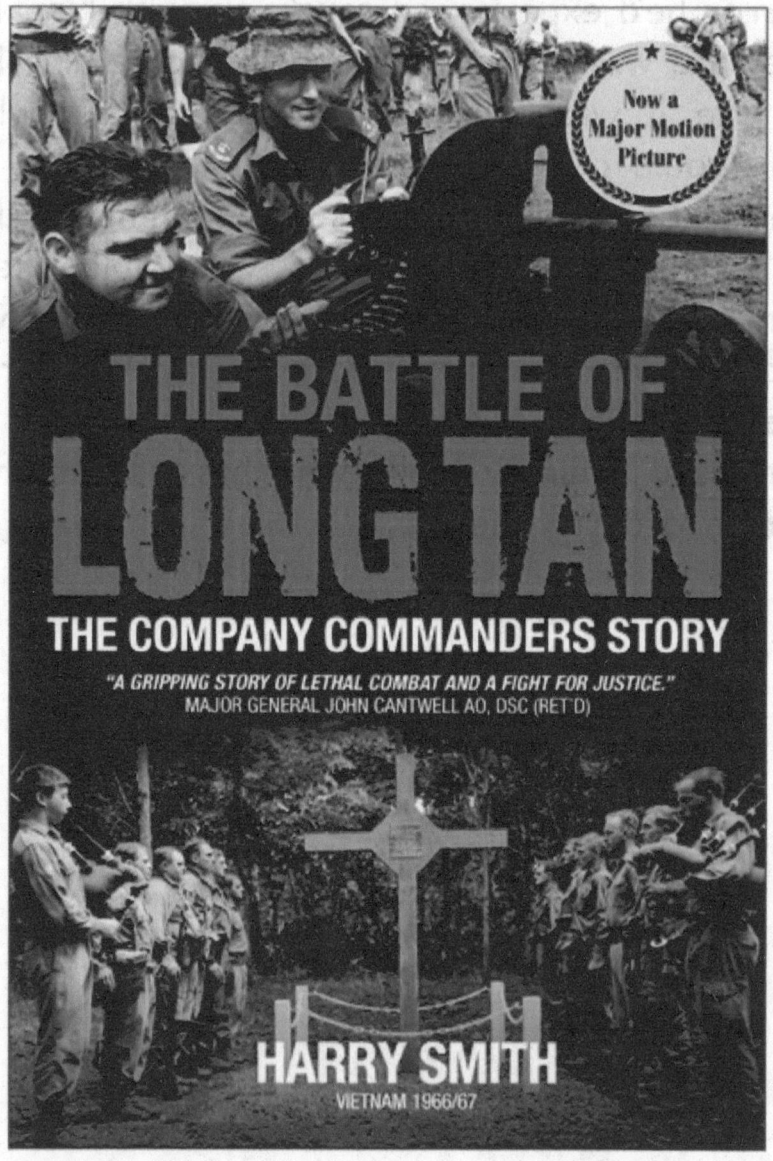

View sample pages, reviews and more information on this and other titles at www.bigskypublishing.com.au

Long Listed for ABIA Publishers' Adult Book of the Year

On the afternoon of 18 August 1966, just five kilometres from their main Australian Task Force base at Nui Dat, a group of Viet Cong soldiers walked into the right flank of Delta Company 6 RAR. Under a blanket of mist and heavy monsoon rain, amid the mud and shattered rubber trees, a dispersed Company of 108 men held its ground with courage and grim determination against a three-sided attack from a force of 2,500 Viet Cong and North Vietnamese Army troops.

When the battle subsided, 18 Australian soldiers lay dead and 24 had been wounded. Battlefield clearance revealed 245 enemy bodies with captured documents later confirming the count at over 500 enemy killed and 800 wounded.

These men were led by a gruff and gutsy perfectionist Major Harry Smith. Now some 50 years after the battle, Harry tells his story. Long Tan is more than just an account of a historic battle. Harry Smith takes his readers on an extraordinary journey – one that ultimately reveals a remarkable coverup at the highest military and political echelons.

Written in partnership with award-winning journalist Toni McRae, Long Tan is also Harry's

Long Listed for Small Publishers' Adult Book of the Year 2016

On the afternoon of 18 August 1966, just five kilometres from the main Australian Task Force base at Nui Dat, a group of Viet Cong soldiers walked into the right flank of Delta Company, 6 RAR. Under a blanket of mist and heavy monsoon rain, amid the mud and shattered rubber trees, a dispersed Company of 108 men held its ground with courage and grim determination against a three-sided attack from a force of 2,500 Viet Cong and North Vietnamese Army troops.

When the battle subsided, 18 Australian soldiers lay dead and 24 had been wounded. Battlefield clearance revealed 245 enemy bodies with captured documents later confirming the count at over 500 enemy killed and 800 wounded.

These men were led by a gruff and gusty perfectionist, Major Harry Smith. Now, some 50 years after the battle, Harry tells his story. Long Tan is more than just an account of a historic battle. Harry Smith takes his readers on an extraordinary journey—one that ultimately reveals a remarkable cover-up at the highest military and political echelons.

Written in partnership with award-winning journalist Toni McRae, Long Tan is also Harry's life story and portrays his many personal battles, from failed marriages to commando-style killing; from a horrific parachute accident through to his modern-day struggles with bureaucracy for recognition for his soldiers. Harry's battles are tempered by his love of sailing, where he has at last found some peace.

Long Tan portrays the wrenching, visceral experience of a man who has fought lifelong battles, in a story that he is only now able to tell. Harry can still hear the gunfire and smell the blood spilt at Long Tan. For him, the fight continues.

Available now online or at all good bookstores

View sample pages, reviews and more information on this and other titles at www.bigskypublishing.com.au

Indal M. Sshu, the history of Australian navigator Oscar Furmist and of 55,000 young men who perished while flying for Bomber Command during World War II. Lovingly crafted by his nephew, Mat Elliott, this book brings to life a young man whose name was never spoken by his family and who was a stranger to his modern-day descendants.

Elliott follows Oscar from his earliest childhood in the Blue Mountains through his training over the vast expanses of Canada to the mist-shrouded patchwork landscape of Britain and on to the hostile skies of occupied France. He uses the accounts of the two surviving aircrew to piece together the events of the fateful night that saw most of the crew of Lancaster JA70's affectionally know as 'Naughty Nan', perish as pilot Colin Dickson heroically manoeuvred his burning aircraft away from the towns and villages that dotted the landscape. This has been a difficult book for Elliott to write as it contains a harrowing description of his uncle's last moments. The terrible impact of the deaths of the aircrew are vividly described alongside the miraculous tales of the two survivors.

But for the family of Oscar Furmist there would be no miracle, just the lingering weight of deep and lasting grief. This is a story that moves beyond the technical descriptions of bombing

Fatal Mission is the story of Australian navigator Oscar Furniss, just one of 55,000 young men who perished while flying for Bomber Command during World War II. Lovingly crafted by his nephew, Mal Elliott, this book brings to life a young man whose name was never spoken by his family and who was a stranger to his modern-day descendants.

Elliott follows Oscar from his carefree childhood in the Blue Mountains through his training over the vast emptiness of Canada to the mist-shrouded patchwork landscapes of Britain and on to the hostile skies of occupied France. He uses the accounts of the two surviving aircrew to piece together the events of the fateful night that saw most of the crew of Lancaster JA901, affectionately know as Naughty Nan, perish as pilot Colin Dickson heroically manoeuvred his burning aircraft away from the towns and villages that dotted the landscape. This has been a difficult book for Elliott to write as it contains a harrowing description of his uncle's last moments. The terrible impact of the deaths of the aircrew are vividly described alongside the miraculous tales of the two survivors.

But for the family of Oscar Furniss there would be no miracle, just the lingering weight of deep and lasting grief. This is a story that moves beyond the technical descriptions of bombing missions to describe the human toll of conflict. It underlines the crucial importance of commemoration, of refusing to allow those who perished in war to be forgotten. Theirs was a sacrifice that we who live in freedom should never forget.

Available now online or at all good bookstores

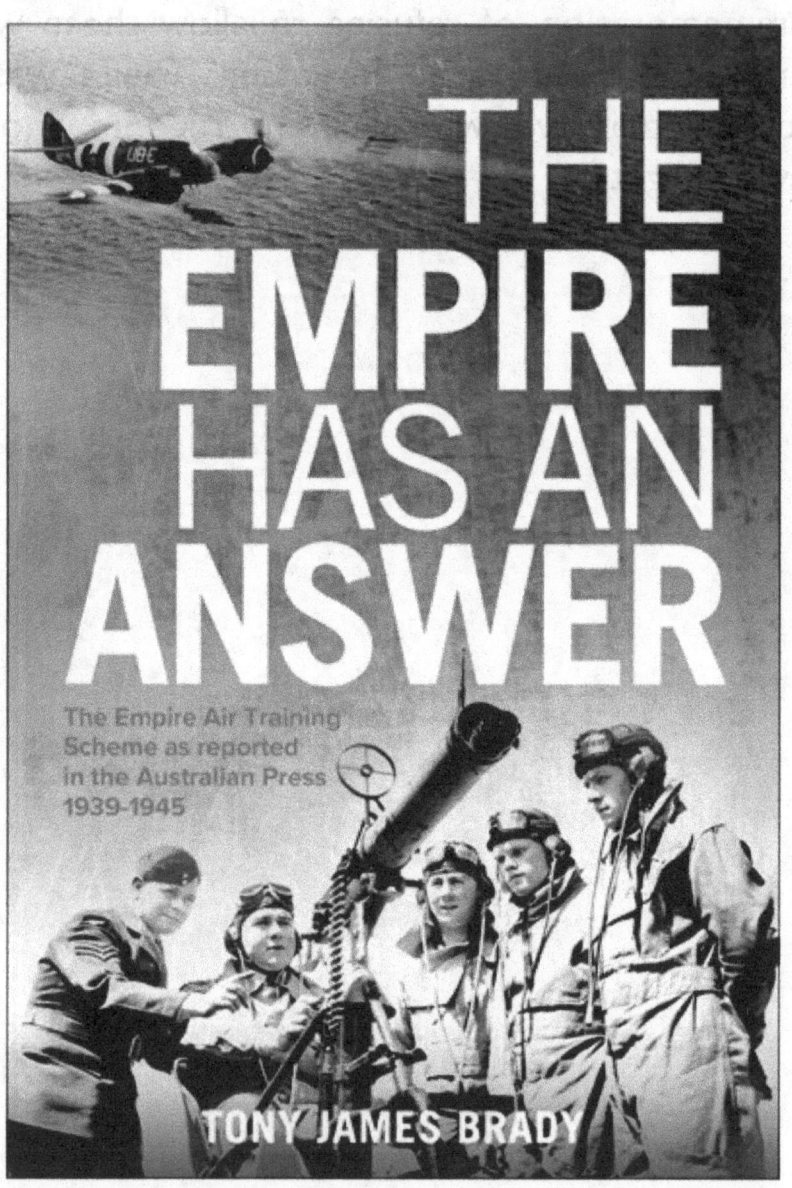

View sample pages, reviews and more information on this and other titles at www.bigskypublishing.com.au

'IF WE DO NOT WIN THE BATTLE OF TRAINING, WE SHALL WIN NO OTHER BATTLE IN THE AIR.'

In 1943 the Royal Air Force recognised that training a vast amount of aircrew for a high attrition war was essential to an Allied victory, and that the key to winning the 'battle of training' was the Empire Air Training Scheme (EATS).

37,576 Australian aircrew graduated from the EATS. Over 300 were killed whilst training for war and 9874 aircrew were killed or listed as missing while on active duty. Those who fought under this scheme during World War II amounted to just 6.7 per cent of Australian service personnel serving overseas yet the aircrew losses amounted to almost 25 per cent of all the Australian fatalities during the war. This made serving in EATS among the most hazardous duties of the war.

The Empire has an Answer was researched using more than 35,000 articles, from 50 metropolitan, regional, and district newspapers, and what materialised was a story of one of, if not, the greatest training programs the world has seen.

Follow the journey from the conception and implementation of the scheme, through recruitment and basic training, flight training, and then into combat. The individual accounts woven into the narrative provide a first-hand experience of the triumphs and trials of typical airmen and airwomen who performed extraordinary feats in a time of great need.

The significant achievements and success of the Empire Air Training Scheme has for the most part been overlooked in our history, until now.

BACK COVER MATERIAL

'THERE'S THE BEND IN THE ROAD AT LONG TAN,' I SAID. 'WE'RE BEHIND ENEMY LINES. TURN BACK EAST, QUICKLY'. I HAD BEEN SCARED BEFORE BUT NOW I WAS TERRIFIED.

In 1966, Bob Grandin was a Royal Australian Airforce helicopter pilot stationed in Vietnam. This book is written from the logbook he kept while working in Nui Dat and is a fascinating Look at life during war – the dangers, the challenges and the mundaneness.

On 18 August he was co-pilot on a 9 Squadron Iroquois 'Huey' helicopter that flew over the enemy to resupply desperate solders engaged in battle at the Long Tan rubber plantation. Enduring extremely poor weather conditions and enemy fire the critical role played by Bob and 9 Squadron in the Battle of Long Tan contributed to the success of this battle.

The narrative of his war experiences are interwoven with stories of his life after Vietnam, revealing the difficulties he faced back home, the impact of the war on his psyche and relationships, and his struggles with PTSD.

A collection of Australian newspaper articles saved by Bob's father feature throughout, giving further insight into how important helicopters were in Viernam, and also how the press reported the war to the Australian public.

Answering the Call provides the unique perspective of a wartime helicopter pilot and is an important addition to Vietnam War history

www.ingramcontent.com/pod-product-compliance
Lightning Source LLC
Chambersburg PA
CBHW010718300426
44114CB00022B/2888